Endorsements

Well, well done! This book is beautiful, encouraging, and relatable. I'm a better momma for having read it. Thank you.
—*Mikaela Mathews,* writing coach and editor, mom of two

I love how relatable each of the devotions is to my own life! I can see myself in almost all these scenarios!
—*Natalie Scott,* teacher, mom of two

For a young mama, this book is a rare gem! There is such honesty, rawness, and practical guidance in this. Lynn is a mama who has been there and done that, providing a wealth of knowledge for moms of all ages.
—*Elene Banks,* founder of Christian Mompreneurs, business owner, mom of four

I wish I had had this devotional study thirty years ago! As a working mom, I can attest to the personal and professional demands in every phase of mom life. Lynn opens her heart and provides tools to encourage women of all ages to develop a closer relationship with Jesus through the power of Scripture layered with personal experiences that help us navigate the joys and struggles of being a mom.
—*Trisha Cunningham,* nonprofit CEO and former corporate executive, mom of two

HOME RUN! Wow, Lynn hit it out of the park! I connected with every single story she shared, as I find myself walking incredibly similar issues in so many ways! This Bible study could not have come at a more opportune time in my life. Thank you, Lynn!
—*Dr. Cortney Baker,* CEO/KidsCare Home Health, mom of three

Through thoughtful journaling questions and engaging devotions, Lynn helps each of us see how God was faithful earlier in our lives and has been faithful through Scripture, teaching us to trust that God will show himself faithful again, no matter what the circumstances of our lives.

—*Christie Thomas,* award-winning author of *Fruit Full: 100 Family Experiences for Growing in the Fruit of the Spirit,* mom of three

These encouraging devotionals challenged me to remember all that God has done in my own life. Lynn shares her heart through each story. You will be inspired!

—*Dr. Melissa Ewing,* Dallas Baptist University adjunct professor, mom of three, grandma to one

Thank you for this twenty-one-day challenge! It is an excellent resource that encapsulates spiritual sustenance and foundational biblical truths to encourage and strengthen moms striving to finish the race that God has called her to.

—*Rhonda Brittain,* Minister to Preschool at Prestonwood Baptist Church, mom of three and Lolli to four

Faithful before Faithful again

FINDING GOD FAITHFUL IN AN ANXIOUS WORLD

Melissa —

Thank you for encouraging me to share whatever God gave me for his holy purposes!

Lynn

Ps. See you on TikTok 🙂

A 21 DAY CHALLENGE

Faithful before Faithful again

FINDING GOD FAITHFUL IN AN ANXIOUS WORLD

LYNN NITCHER

REDEMPTION PRESS

© 2024 by Lynn Nitcher. All rights reserved.

Published by Redemption Press, PO Box 427, Enumclaw, WA 98022.
Toll-Free (844) 2REDEEM (273-3336)

Redemption Press is honored to present this title in partnership with the author. The views expressed or implied in this work are those of the author. Redemption Press provides our imprint seal representing design excellence, creative content, and high-quality production.

Noncommercial interests may reproduce portions of this book without the express written permission of the author, provided the text does not exceed five hundred words. When reproducing text from this book, include the following credit line: "*Faithful Before, Faithful Again* by Lynn Nitcher. Used by permission."

Commercial interests: No part of this publication may be reproduced in any form, stored in a retrieval system, or transmitted in any form by any means—electronic, photocopy, recording, or otherwise—without prior written permission of the publisher/author, except as provided by United States of America copyright law.

Unless otherwise indicated, all Scripture quotations are from The Holy Bible, New International Version®, NIV® copyright © 1973, 1978, 1984, 2011 by Biblica, Inc.® Used by permission. All rights reserved worldwide.

Scripture quotations marked (ESV) are from The ESV® Bible (The Holy Bible, English Standard Version®), copyright © 2001 by Crossway, a publishing ministry of Good News Publishers. Used by permission. All rights reserved."

Scripture quotations marked (ASV) are from the American Standard Version of the Bible, which is in the public domain.

Author's photo captured by Meredith Brumwell.

ISBN 13: 978-1-951350-53-6 (Paperback)
978-1-951350-54-3 (ePUB)
Library of Congress Catalog Card Number: 2023913919

TO

Reggie, Amanda, Lacey, Reid, Zach, Dillon,
Nash, Riley, Mom, Dad, and Stacey

So grateful for your love.

Table of Contents

Introduction xi

Day 1	Faithful in Parenting	15
Day 2	Faithful in Anxiety	21
Day 3	Faithful in Temptation	27
Day 4	Faithful in Loss	33
Day 5	Faithful in Busyness	39
Day 6	Faithful in Disappointment	45
Day 7	Faithful in Fear	51
Day 8	Faithful in Presence	57
Day 9	Faithful in Identity	63
Day 10	Faithful in Protection	69
Day 11	Faithful in Conviction	75
Day 12	Faithful in Friendship	81
Day 13	Faithful in Priorities	87
Day 14	Faithful in Uncertainty	93
Day 15	Faithful in Joy	99
Day 16	Faithful in Baggage	105
Day 17	Faithful in Forgiveness	111
Day 18	Faithful in Imperfection	117
Day 19	Faithful in Pride	123
Day 20	Faithful in Intentionality	129
Day 21	Faithful in Encouragement	135

Now What? 139
Endnotes 142

Introduction

I started a new semester of Bible study at church right before the pandemic began and the entire world shut down. The group never started back up, leaving us to finish the study alone at home. Once I completed it, I realized a new church study would not start for another five months. What would I do in the meantime? I had been in this position multiple times through the years, but it sat on my heart differently this time. Had I relegated time with Jesus to a registration link and $20 book fee twice a year?

With prevalent conversations around anxiety in the newfound chaos of 2020, I starting the *Drive Thru Moms* podcast that fall to share stories of God's goodness and extraordinary work in ordinary moms. But God began to remind me of another seed he had previously planted—to spend more time alone with him. So in early fall of 2021, I paused actively recording the *Drive Thru Moms* podcast to limit my distractions so I could better focus on him.

God has been preparing my heart to write this book for years. My oldest interviewed me on my first episode of the *Drive Thru Moms* podcast, and I shared then my heart for writing a book and fulfilling the idea God gave me years ago. I laughed about it when he first planted the seed. *I'm not a writer. What do I know?* But he never let it go.

The more time I spent in my Bible with God, the more he revealed the unhealthy ways I deal with pressures and stress. Was I overwhelmed by my own doing? And what made it better, or at least alleviated, the repercussions of my current load? Who did I truly rely on in the middle of my unsettled seasons? The many challenges I often complained about as a mom, the hurry and busyness of corralling three kids and their activities, cruising through more drive-thru windows than I can count, were reactions to seasons of fear and anxiety. And God was bringing some much-needed clarity.

I've come to believe that I have dealt with anxiety, on some level, my entire life. I have learned to navigate my fears and limit my stressors, while reaching to God for continuous help. And the more time I spend with him, the more peace I feel! Imagine that!

My story isn't any different from millions of moms who deal with anxiety and feelings of being overwhelmed in the mess and chaos of motherhood. But God showed me that though my story may not be different, perhaps my perspective is.

Don't get me wrong, I'm not excluding the value of seeking professional help from a counselor or doctor, prescribed medications, or talks with a trusted, godly friend or pastor. I love my counselor! But God showed me that more often than not, I was trying to handle things all on my own. I was forced to take a look and see the areas I was choosing to inject God's perspective into my life and the areas I was leaving him out.

This 21-day challenge walks through examples of stressors and challenges common to moms, encouraging us to bring anxiety and God to the same intersection—that line where the forest meets the sun. As the book cover indicates, it's a place where the dark path is yet to end, yet light reveals the end of the road. My hope and prayerful desire with this devotional is that moms will

- Personally discover God's past faithfulness
- Begin to develop a daily habit of time in God's presence

Our seasons of motherhood change rapidly. The challenges of today aren't the stressors we will face tomorrow. Will we handle future anxious moments in fear? Or will we be guided in faith, remembering a God who was faithful before?

Thank you for committing to spend twenty-one days devoted to being in God's presence. Mom life is an amazing privilege, in which we get to shepherd the hearts of the ones God has entrusted to our care. God's Word is powerful to heal our hurts and embolden our faith in him, filling our future with hope, joy, and remembrance of his constant presence.

Consider yourself prayed for,

Lynn

Day One

The main thing is to keep the main thing the main thing.

—Stephen Covey[1]

Day 1

Faithful in Parenting

I was desperate for friends when my oldest was a baby. Though stay-at-home mom life was beautiful—full of freedom, fun, and challenging new experiences—it was also extremely lonely. At the time, my husband traveled regularly, out of town four to five days a week for several years. So I decided to join a Bible study at our new church, a seemingly perfect opportunity to make friends and spend time with the Lord.

God used this time in an unexpected way. Aside from gaining new mom friends and wisdom from those who were further down the parenting road, this Bible study showed me how much I had to learn. Growing up in church, I thought I had a good grip on the Bible, but I began to discover what the Bible had to say about the importance of teaching our children.

> Hear, O Israel: The Lord our God, the Lord is one. Love the Lord your God with all your heart and with all your soul and with all your strength. These commandments that I give you today are to be on your hearts. Impress them on your children. Talk about them when you sit at home and when you walk along the road, when you lie down and when you get up. Tie them as symbols on your hands and bind them on your foreheads. Write them on the doorframes of your houses and on your gates. (Deuteronomy 6:4–9)

Exposed to so much Scripture I had never considered before, I began to feel overwhelmed. *Can I teach my daughter what I don't know?* (And there was *so* much to know!) Learning more about the Bible and imparting God's lessons quickly became my number one priority to prepare my baby girl for the adult world. That sounds great in theory, I'll admit. But for someone with a perfectionistic, type A personality mixed with an anxious tendency to take a deep dive into minutia, I struggled for years with the insecurity that I would never have all the answers.

I'm supposed to have all the answers, right? God graciously answered that question for me through a conversation with a friend. My massage therapist apologized profusely as she opened the door, running fifteen minutes late. I had been seeing this massage therapist, and now friend, for about ten years. Running late was very unusual for her, so I asked if everything was okay. Her response surprised me.

"Yes, I've just been talking about Jesus all day and ran over on all of my appointments!" she said.

I could feel her love for Christ. Though we chitchatted about other parts of her life, she asked me questions I will never forget: "What is the difference between the Old and New Testaments? And can you tell me about the Holy Spirit? How are they all three yet one person?" In that moment, two things hit me:

1) God spoke through me! I shared explanations and gave examples I had forgotten I even knew, listening to myself in a sort of out-of-body experience. I explained the Bible as a love story from start to finish—Old to New Testament—and how it fit together. To be honest, I don't remember everything I said!
2) I don't have to know everything. This dear friend was sharing the love of Christ day in and day out as a new believer and had no idea the difference between the Old Testament and the New Testament. God reminded me he is still the one who fills in my lack. It's okay to not know it all.

My friend had yet to discover the beautiful threads woven through the tapestry of God's Word. She was simply excited about Jesus and his forgiveness! That's what it's all about! "The devil is in the details" describes my mind, often holding me at first base and keeping me from advancing to second. There is no way this side of heaven I will ever be able to completely understand or impart the fullness of Scripture to my children, or to anyone else for that matter. God simply showed me that he wants me to share his love and forgiveness and not live in fear of not knowing it all. Our self-inflicted notion of being all things to all people—or at the very least to "our people"—is a mental spiral the Enemy uses to defeat and discourage us.

I've witnessed other young moms going through the same struggles I dealt with years ago as a young mom. As an administrative assistant and office manager through the years, my office became a refuge for these young women walking the same path I had for years. (I now understood why a former assistant principal I worked with kept chocolates and tissues in her office.)

Conversations with other moms at work, at church, and in my social circles often revolved around concerns like, Can I be the mom, wife, cook, chauffeur, leader, daughter, friend, and housekeeper I want to be while being physically fit, enjoying a hobby, working, running a business, and spiritually leading my children? How on earth can I know all the things and teach my kids when I can barely find time to take a bath or do my hair?

God used this season to show me I had made it through with his help, and now I had the opportunity to pay it forward. I found myself encouraging other moms. "You will be okay." "No, you can't do it all, and that's where God comes in!"

> I lift up my eyes to the mountains—where does my help come from? My help comes from the Lord, the Maker of heaven and earth. (Psalm 121:1–2)

In Deuteronomy 6, God reminds his people—the Jews—that he is their supreme source of strength. He commands them to pass that belief to their children. Matthew 5:17 also reminds us that Christ came to fulfill the law, because no one can ever know it all, much less keep it all.

Christ's new command in John 13:31–34 tells us to love God and love others, and it shows us God's desired focus for our hearts. Our weaknesses or inadequacies in parenting aren't something to fixate on, but rather they are opportunities to look to God as our source of strength in the gaps. It's not about the entirety of what we know but the sovereignty of *who* we know.

As a dear friend used to say in our daily morning meetings, our priority is in "pointing littles to Jesus." God will do as he promised. He will give us wisdom when we ask for it (James 1) and direct our paths in the way we should go (Proverbs 3:5–6, Psalm 37:23–25), leading as all good shepherds do (Psalm 23).

Reflecting on God's Faithfulness

Faithful Before: Can you look back at a season in your parenting where you saw God's faithfulness to give you wisdom? Write about it here, thanking him for his goodness.

_____

_____

_____

_____

His Word: Read Deuteronomy 6:4–9, Luke 10:25–28, and John 13:34–35. Write out what God asks of us and what we are to also teach our children.

_____

_____

_____

_____

Faithful Again: Are you currently struggling in a difficult parenting season? Write out a prayer, asking him to remind you of his promise to always be with you.

_____

_____

_____

_____

#faithfulbeforefaithfulagain   DAY 1: Faithful in Parenting

Day Two

Anxiety is a lot like a toddler. It never stops talking, tells you you're wrong about everything, and wakes you up at 3 a.m.

—*Anonymous*[2]

Day 2

Faithful in Anxiety

Millions of people devoured the best-selling book *Where the Crawdads Sing*. I, however, was not one of them. I tried but just could not get into it. The beginning of the book and movie tell a backstory of a young girl's life, full of abuse, hardship, and poverty. That portion proved difficult to read for my often G-rated heart. Yet somehow I still was enticed to the theater to see it play on the big screen with my mom and best friend.

At the beginning of what ends up as a sweet friendship between the shopkeeper (known as Jumpin'), his wife, and the main character (Kya), two simple words stuck in my craw. (Sorry, I couldn't help myself!) *Be careful.*

An elementary-aged Kya arrives in the general store alone. Her obvious need for adult supervision only pales in comparison to her clear lack of food or shoes. Jumpin' and his wife exchange glances, ultimately analyzing the situation differently, and he warns his wife, "Be careful."

Sounds simple enough. *Be careful.* A phrase we hear every day. But it was the wife's answer that intrigued me, leaving me to mull over the effect these two words so often have on my own anxious heart. "It don't say that in the Bible. Be careful. 'And the king shall answer and say unto them, "Verily I shall say unto thee, in as much as ye have done it unto to the least of these, my brethren, you have done it unto me."' Don't say nothin' about be careful."[3]

Jumpin' reminds his wife that their interference in helping a young girl who appears to manage surviving on her own could make matters worse. Getting involved in a messy situation could be dangerous, starting something they might later regret. What if the father became angry with them?

There's the rub!

It's the what-if questions that cause us to pause and instill doubt and fear, instead of a million-and-one possible positive outcomes.

Don't get me wrong. There are times for quick reminders from those who love us most and who have a vested interest in our well-being. A quick "be careful" to your traveling daughter on the road alone or to someone running to the store after dark by themselves are words often spoken in justified concern. Our mom hearts appear to be in the right place. But shouldn't those admonishments, especially to our children, be filtered through the sieve of courage and wisdom, which God laid out in Scripture? Wouldn't encouraging someone to "drive safely" be preferable to planting a seed of fear for all the possible things that could go wrong? Encouraging our children to face opportunities and obstacles through a biblical lens can alleviate anxiety, which often accompanies the unknown.

The best way to combat underlying fear is to start with God's Word. Talking with a trusted friend, therapist, or counselor can also play a vital role in working through anxious thoughts. But regular study of God's Word instills peace, revealing it is not all up to us. And when we teach our children to turn to the Lord and dig out what Scripture says, he reveals his truth to us. His Word gives us the tools to fight the lies the Enemy throws at us day in and day out.

Scripture is full of encouragement. Proverbs guides us in where to find wisdom. The first chapter in Joshua reminds us that God will never leave us, and it incites us to be courageous (a personal favorite). In Paul's letter to the church in Corinth, he reminds the Corinthians to stand firm in what they know to be true (1 Corinthians 16:13).

To be fair, yes, the Bible does warn the reader to be careful. But those references point to the need for God's wisdom, allowing us to mindfully tuck it away for just such occasions:

> Above all else, *guard your heart,* for everything you do flows from it. (Proverbs 4:23, emphasis added)

> *Choose my instruction* instead of silver, knowledge rather than choice gold. (Proverbs 8:10, emphasis added)

> But *be very careful* to keep the commandment and the law that Moses the servant of the Lord gave you: to love the Lord your

> God, to walk in obedience to him, to keep his commands, to hold fast to him and to serve him with all your heart and with all your soul. (Joshua 22:5, emphasis added)

These verses, and others, point us to fully devoting ourselves to God and recognizing him as our source of strength. Looking at life through an anxious lens blurs what God's Word promises for us as believers in Christ … peace.

> Do not be anxious about anything, but in every situation by prayer and petition, with thanksgiving, present your requests to God. And the peace of God, which transcends all understanding, will guard your hearts and your minds in Christ Jesus. (Philippians 4:6–7)

Recognizing God's past faithfulness sustains us in new and trying situations. By taking Scripture to heart, we can trust God's love for us and daily remind ourselves of his purpose and intention for our life on earth, even in the mundane. May Jesus's words provide us comfort: "I have told you these things, so that in me you may have peace. In this world, you will have trouble. But take heart! I have overcome the world" (John 16:33).

Will we face decisions that cause us to pause to consider our options? Of course! We live in a struggle-filled, sinful, and self-absorbed world. As moms, it's important how we frame those times while our children are still in our care. We can either promote fear and worry, based on past cynical or anxious experiences, or empower the greatest loves of our lives in the Spirit.

Encouraging our kids to find peace in following an all-powerful Father, who is loving and waiting with open arms, readies them for each new dilemma that comes their way.

Reflecting on God's Faithfulness

Faithful Before: Can you remember a season when anxiety kept you from trusting in God first? Write about it here, thanking him for his goodness to walk with you.

_____

_____

_____

_____

His Word: Read 1 Peter 5:6–7 and write it out below.

_____

_____

_____

_____

Faithful Again: Are you currently struggling with anxiety in a particular aspect of your life? Write out a prayer, and ask God to remind you of his presence now.

_____

_____

_____

_____

#faithfulbeforefaithfulagain   DAY 2: Faithful in Anxiety

Day Three

If you will tell me when God permits a Christian to lay aside his armour, I will tell you when Satan has left off temptation.

—*Charles H. Spurgeon*[4]

Day 3

Faithful in Temptation

Once a year, our family drives to a lake a couple of hours from home for a long weekend getaway. Living in a large metropolitan area has its perks, but traffic, noise, and congestion aren't among them. This particular year we ventured back to one of our favorite spots—a lake surrounded by tall pine trees, hiking trails, and streams that beg you to jump in.

In all transparency, we are not an outdoorsy bunch. When our kids were growing up, most of our weekend activities consisted of gymnastics meets, baseball games, and church-related activities. The closest we got to the great outdoors included Gatorade, pop-ups tents, and foldout chairs on the sidelines.

As the kids got older, we tried out some new activities, discovering that we all love the beach, and my boys enjoyed snow-covered ski adventures. But lake life grew on us, allowing us to enjoy a new aspect of the great outdoors. Plus, with one married, one in college, and one about to graduate from high school at the time, we saw the writing on the wall. We wanted to be together as a family as much as possible before our kids started their own families.

One day as the boys were fishing, the girls and I tagged along to sunbathe along the stream's banks at the backside of the dam. We walked the long and winding, tree-lined path into the woods. It was full of rocks and roots and required our full attention to not trip.

While the boys searched for a peaceful landing spot for the morning, the girls and I stretched out on beach towels close by so we could watch them fish. Away from the noise of the city, roads, and dam above, we had stepped into the peace and quiet of Ouachita forest, with not a soul around. Just us.

My husband, son, and son-in-law approached the water with their latest lures and other slimy gadgets. About forty-five minutes into their casting rhythm, three teenagers disrupted our serene retreat, choosing a jumping and swimming spot right next to my son. The fish became scarce with each of their jumps, and they seemed oblivious to their own noise and interruption. My son, on the other hand, was fully aware. He looked up at me wide-eyed and perturbed, and with shoulders lifted, his hands gestured to me as if to say, "What the heck?"

> No temptation has overtaken you that is not common to man. God is faithful, and he will not let you be tempted beyond your ability, but with the temptation he will also provide the way of escape, that you may be able to endure it. (1 Corinthians 10:13 ESV)

As I watched the scene unfold, I was struck by his decision to take the high road. He calmly closed and locked his tackle box, picked up his backpack and water bottle, and simply moved to a new spot, away from the noise, splashing, and distraction that might tempt him to retaliate. He didn't provoke a scene or argument.

Talk about good decision-making in action. My son recognized a situation that could have tempted him to react in a less than Christlike manner, so he changed direction. It was beautiful. A tempting situation handled with such grace and self-control. Let's be honest. He got it from his dad.

As moms, we are no strangers to emotions that cloud our judgment. We fall prey to our own devices, replying often in our flesh and lashing out, instead of listening to the Holy Spirit's whisper that there is another way. "Submit yourselves, then, to God. Resist the devil, and he will flee from you" (James 4:7).

Watching my son recognize the irritant and choose to listen to the Holy Spirit was poignant and especially convicting to my mom heart. As moms, our reactions are witnessed by the children entrusted to us, and I freely admit, I fail miserably at this at times. A snarky comment to my husband here or there. Words or attitudes in anger and frustration. Can you relate?

In 1 Corinthians 10, Paul warns the church in Corinth about Israel's disobedience, reminding them of past generations. The children of Israel had witnessed the acts of God:

the Red Sea's division, salvation from Pharaoh and his armies, protection and provision for years in the desert. Before Moses died, he reminded the children of Israel of said provisions (Deuteronomy 29:5). Along their forty-year journey in the wilderness, their clothes and sandals never wore out and their feet never swelled. But their parents and grandparents complained, turned to sin, and lost permission to enter the promised land they had been delivered from Egypt to enjoy. Dying in the wilderness ahead of the next generation that would inherit the land, Moses reminded this new generation of their faithful God.

Were they forgetful? Why were they so sinful? Opportunity after opportunity found them with a choice: Remember God's faithfulness with gratitude, or get stuck on the trouble at hand? They were sick of manna and complained, even though God provided for them every day. They were tired of the journey, even though God had delivered them from slavery in Egypt. They wanted to see a physical god, even though God protected them from the heat of the day with clouds and warmed them with fire above at night. They lost sight of God's goodness and provision at every turn, running to the immediate thing that satisfied them … self.

Isn't that how we are tempted? Are we any different?

So what do we do instead? Scripture makes it clear. "We demolish arguments and every pretension that sets itself up against the knowledge of God, and we take captive every thought to make it obedient to Christ" (2 Corinthians 10:5).

Let us be ever waiting to hear from God, with hearts so tender to his voice we recognize thoughts of doubt or anger not from God that tempt us to sin. Our goal is to squelch anything that doesn't align with his holiness, before we react in our human desires of self-fulfillment. God's wisdom and provision to escape temptation bring beauty and show his faithfulness to care for us, just as he did with the Israelites. (Sidenote, who says the Old Testament is irrelevant and boring? I love it all!)

Pausing in a tempting situation and stopping a reaction that is less than holy frees us to listen for the Holy Spirit's direction. We can pack our tackle box and move to another spot, freed to cast elsewhere, unobstructed by noisy irritants, and able to draw closer to God's heart and hear his voice.

Reflecting on God's Faithfulness

Faithful Before: Can you look back and see how God has walked you through a season of temptation and provided a way of escape? Write about it here, thanking him for seeing you through.

_____

_____

_____

_____

His Word: Write out 1 Corinthians 10:13.

_____

_____

_____

_____

Faithful Again: Are you currently struggling with a distraction or temptation in a particular aspect of your life? Write out a prayer thanking God for his previous provision and asking him for guidance.

_____

_____

_____

_____

Day Four

How lucky I am to have something that makes saying goodbye so hard.

—A. A. Milne[5]

Day 4

Faithful in Loss

I'm embarrassed to admit I was a tiny bit relieved when I woke up to light rain one morning, which could potentially postpone the day's event.

I planned to attend a balloon launch with several friends to honor those who had suffered the loss of a child, regardless of age, development, or circumstances. A silent auction at the event would raise funds to support these grieving families. It was a small way to help a grieving friend. However my reticence in attending the event was more involved than I was willing to admit.

A close friend and I drove together and met up with our friends. We hugged, cried, took pictures, and walked the grounds looking at the silent auction on display. The number of people in attendance surprised me and weighed heavily, evidence of so much loss. When the time came, those who had experienced the loss of a child launched a balloon in memory of their lost loved one.

People cried and wrote the names of their children on the balloons, as if to kiss them to heaven when they released them into the clouds. At first I just stood there, a frozen bystander, stuffing down my own feelings and thinking, *I'm just here to support*. It was then that my friend took my hand and said, "Don't you want to get two balloons?" I shook my head no, as tears threatened to spill. My friend and I worked closely together, and I had shared my story with her somewhere along the way.

I was born with physical problems that instilled fear I would never have children. I had to trust God with my deep desire for children before my husband and I were even married. But God, as so often ends up being the case, allowed me to become pregnant anyway. Not once, but five times.

Two of those pregnancies ended in loss, and it wasn't until that day at the balloon launch that I realized how those losses still affected me some twenty-five years later. Even then, with a married daughter, one in college, and one about to graduate from high school, I was a blubbering mess.

In John 19, John describes himself as "the disciple whom Jesus loved." After three years of Jesus's earthly ministry, he revealed that it was time to depart, his death imminent. But even with impending suffering, death, and separation from his earthly cohorts, Jesus reflected on his mother. While hanging on the cross, bleeding and suffering and in excruciating pain, knowing the end was at hand, Jesus thought of his mother. Let that sink in for a moment. He thought of his mother while nailed to a cross. Summoning the strength and energy to speak to his mother, in earshot of John, Christ made his wishes known. Based on the care and love he desired for the woman who had sacrificed her reputation and public perception in the strangest way, he remembered how she would suffer again. And Jesus knew the devastation and sadness that was coming. But he made a way: "When Jesus saw his mother there, and the disciple whom he loved standing nearby, he said to her, 'Women, here is your son,' and to the disciple, 'Here is your mother.' From that time on, this disciple took her into his home" (John 19:26–27).

Jesus knew the loss she would feel. A separation, even if not permanent, is still a separation. As fully God, yet fully man, Jesus understood the depth of our emotions and felt them deeply. When he watched dear friends suffer loss when their brother Lazarus died, "Jesus wept" (John 11:35), knowing he would raise Lazarus from the dead. He didn't rush to end their tears; he let them grieve. "The Lord is close to the brokenhearted and saves those who are crushed in spirit" (Psalm 34:18).

Jesus created a plan to protect, provide, and assist his mother in his absence. But he didn't stop there. Before his departure, he reassured his disciples, who had traveled with him on his gospel-spreading journey, that he would not leave them on their own. He would indeed send a Comforter. "And I will pray the Father, and he shall give you another Comforter, that he may be with you forever" (John 14:16 ASV). The Holy Spirit would come to direct, guide, and comfort the disciples in the loss of their Savior.

Friend, our loss does not go unnoticed by the Father. Even after all these years, my heart still grieves and wonders, as do so many who have experienced the loss of a child, parent, spouse, or friend. Opportunities to love someone in a season of loss are all around us. If we open our eyes and hearts to his leading, God can use us to love them because of his love for us. Walking alongside, crying, or asking a friend if they want a balloon to release brings physical comfort from an unseen yet very real Father. We can take heart in a Comforter who is with us, one who supports us, befriends us, heals us, and restores us to a place of testimony to his goodness … if we let him.

I honestly can't remember if I released those two balloons that day or not. But I left praising the Father for seeing me in my pain, comforting my heart through the words of a friend, and loving my little ones until we are joined together again in heaven. And I can't wait.

Reflecting on God's Faithfulness

Faithful Before: Can you look back and see where God comforted you during a season of loss? Write about it here, thanking him for his goodness.

_____

_____

_____

_____

His Word: Write out Psalm 34:18 or John 14:16 below.

_____

_____

_____

_____

Faithful Again: Are you currently struggling with loss in a particular aspect of your life? Or is there someone close to you in need of support? Write out a prayer asking God to help you feel his comfort and nearness.

_____

_____

_____

_____

#faithfulbeforefaithfulagain

Day Five

There cannot be a crisis next week. My schedule is already full.

—Henry Kissinger[6]

Day 5

Faithful in Busyness

As a former administrative assistant at a large private preschool, one of my tasks was to purchase all the instructional goodies requested by our teaching staff. That meant I had to do a lot of shopping.

Some trips were next level, requiring extra hands and carts. Supplies for more than 240 preschoolers and sixty-plus teachers made a person choosing their checkout lane rethink their position behind me.

This particular trip was a small one, so I was alone. I don't recall the specifics of my purchase, only that I was able to carry the bags to the car and leave my cart in the store before I walked out through the automatic doors.

As I got about halfway to the parking lot, I noticed a quarter on the ground, right in my path. I paused and considered my options. Realizing my hands were too full to pick up the coin, I marched on to my car. I mean, it was a quarter, after all! Setting the bags in the back seat, I drove back to the office, letting the out-of-reach quarter bother me more than twenty-five cents should.

I put away the items in our storage room, sat back at my desk, and began sorting receipts to document my purchase. But the thought of my full hands and hurry to get back to work tumbled around in my mind.

I have not ever heard the Lord's voice out loud in an audible way, where others would be able to hear him talking to me. But I do hear him a lot in the quiet, everyday moments, like the quarter situation. When I take time to listen, it makes room for the Holy Spirit to work.

At that moment, the Lord reminded me of his goodness, if only my hands had been free and if I had available capacity at the moment. He offers goodness for the taking, but it's so often missed. Maybe that's a reach for those of you reading this. I mean, it was just a coin in the parking lot of a local store, for goodness' sake. But God's still voice convicts my heart like that and reveals my tendencies. He's not harsh or authoritarian, but he reveals himself through simple statements in love.

When it comes to carrying bags, I belong to the school of thought that you carry them all at once. Multiple trips are for the faint of heart and weak of arms. Truly, my husband never understands that, always encouraging me to just make a second trip. I also often overload myself in other ways, with commitments and a schedule no one can keep, regardless of my intention. Overcommitment tends to be a recurring theme in my life. It's in that max-capacity mode that we drown out the Holy Spirit's quiet whisper and eliminate wiggle room in our day for God-sized opportunities.

The last thing I want to be is so busy that I can't make time for a conversation with the Lord. To be so busy that I don't even hear his voice in the parking lot. To be so consumed with my thoughts, lists, and social media that I crowd out time with him. That time spent with him directly affects time spent with others on his behalf. And time spent with others, isn't that what we're here for?

In the book of 1 Samuel, we read that Hannah is childless. During a season of intense prayer, she makes a promise to the Lord, vowing to dedicate her son to a life of service to God if he allows her to have one. Soon after, she becomes pregnant. As promised, Hannah takes her son, Samuel, to the temple at the time of the appointed yearly sacrifice. She leaves him in the charge of Eli the priest, giving her son—her answer to prayer—back to the Lord. Samuel stayed there under Eli's care to grow and serve in the temple.

One night when Eli and Samuel were down for the night, Samuel kept hearing a voice calling him. Not yet familiar with the voice of the Lord, he mistook it for the voice of Eli. By the third time he approached Eli to ask why he was calling for him, Eli realized it must be the voice of the Lord.

> Then Eli realized that the LORD was calling the boy. So Eli told Samuel, "Go and lie down, and if he calls you, say, 'Speak, LORD, for your servant is listening.'" So Samuel went and lay down in his place. (1 Samuel 3:8–9)

It wasn't that Samuel didn't hear the voice; obviously, he did. Each time he heard his name, Samuel went in to Eli, the closest one to him. He acknowledged the call and asked what Eli needed. He heard the voice, but he just attributed it to the wrong person. God the Father often makes himself known, asking for our attention, never pushing himself on us, and solely giving us the choice to respond.

Every teacher, disciplinarian, and leader knows attention is garnered in the whisper. The power of the pause forces us to stop, come close, and lean in with anticipation of what is next.

> Then a great and powerful wind tore the mountains apart and shattered the rocks before the Lord, but the Lord was not in the wind. After the wind, there was an earthquake, but the Lord was not in the earthquake. After the earthquake came a fire, but the Lord was not in the fire. And after the fire, came a gentle whisper. When Elijah heard it, he pulled his cloak over his face and went out and stood at the mouth of the cave. (1 Kings 19:11–13)

The Bible Study Tools commentary explains this passage beautifully:

> The wind, and earthquake, and fire, did not make him cover his face, but the still voice did. Gracious souls are more affected by the tender mercies of the Lord than by his terrors. The mild voice of him who speaks from the cross, or the mercy seat, is accompanied with peculiar power in taking possession of the heart.[7]

Our lives are so full of work, carpooling, PTA meetings, book clubs, personal goals, kids' athletic endeavors, virtual meetings, church, and let us not forget the ever-evolving social media platforms. None of them in and of themselves are inherently bad. Individually, they are innocuous, each adding varying degrees of value to our lives. But put them all together, and they become the misinterpreted voice above the noise, drowning out the whisper of the Father.

Next trip … I'm taking my bags to the car in a cart.

Reflecting on God's Faithfulness

Faithful Before: Has there been a season in your life where your schedule has prioritized space to hear from God? Write about it here, thanking him for meeting you there.

_____

_____

_____

_____

His Word: God often showed up in overt, visible ways in the Old Testament (e.g. Elijah mentioned above and with Moses in the fiery bush, in the cloud, and in fire leading the Israelites). Read John 15:4–5, 26 and 16:12–15. Write what you learn about hearing from God.

_____

_____

_____

_____

Faithful Again: Do you currently have the bandwidth to hear God's voice in this season of life? Write out an action plan for making room to hear from the Lord in your day.

_____

_____

_____

_____

#faithfulbeforefaithfulagain

Day Six

Our chief want is someone who will inspire us to be what we know we could be.

—*Ralph Waldo Emerson*[8]

Day 6

Faithful in Disappointment

I failed an art class my sophomore year in college, which forced me to change my major. Stupid prerequisite! Failing was not a good look for this child of two educators.

There I said it. I failed.

I had long wanted to be an interior designer, creating beautiful spaces I could only dream about. I knew what I liked and could see color schemes in my head, but mainly I loved figuring out the functionality of a space. I still remember my first college semester-long project, designing a two-thousand-square-foot condo for a single man and his elementary-aged daughter. I began college making all As in my design and theory classes, so I believed this career was meant for me.

Then came freehand art classes. Could I draw? Was sketching in my wheelhouse? That was a hard no. On a typical day in the art studio of the multistory architecture building, my professor would throw a sheet over a rigged clothesline and bunch it up to create billowy lines and curves. Another day he tore up paper bags, crumpled them, and threw them in bonfire fashion in the middle of the floor. Each time, we were given the same directions—use shading only to recreate the image. Much to my chagrin, I still couldn't do it. Fs were becoming a trend in that class. I couldn't pass, and I ultimately had to drop the class.

Fast forward a few years. My empty-nester husband and I were working on a house project, building our very first custom home. Our first design selection meeting was upon us. We pulled up to the office to look through paint and tile samples and flooring, but I could not get out of the car. Even though I was excited to build and design our first, and probably only, custom home, I was frozen. Oh, I was prepared. I had planned each space, visualized each room, and knew exactly what I wanted. I had printouts of documents and pictures of how I visualized each space to show the designer. I was more than ready! But I just sat there, sending my husband, Reggie, in ahead of me, while I remained motionless outside, fearful my ideas and choices would be all wrong. Until that moment, I never realized how much my past college failure had affected me.

I finally convinced myself to walk inside the building. As I began digging through the beautiful samples, full of texture and color, I found myself back in one of my happy places. My sweet husband remained close by and worked on his laptop for eight solid hours. (He's a patient man!) He was an anchor of safety and security, a touchpoint for my ever-reeling self-doubt. I looked to him for thoughts and nods to indicate his preferences, as if he was at Sotheby's, paddle in hand, waving budgetary approval.

The designer offered me a job within the first hour of our appointment. She might have been kidding, but I really didn't care. That word of validation provided a reminder God knew I needed … I'm not a failure. The God of the universe took the time to remind my tentative heart, I've never been the failure my heart once believed. God knew how I felt, saw my hesitancy and physical withdrawal, and encouraged me through the designer and my husband. He had not forgotten the disappointment in my heart from a failed class I still carried, thirty-five years later.

We don't always get what we want or even when we want it. Don't we tell our kids that? Disappointment can be hard and something we waltz right into the future carrying, not looking to God for perspective. Self-perceived failures can affect our decisions, how we feel about our performance as moms, and even how we relate to our children. Feelings of inadequacy can also often lead us to miss the point of Scripture, but God loves us no matter what. "The LORD appeared to us in the past, saying: I have loved you with an everlasting love; I have drawn you with unfailing kindness'" (Jeremiah 31:3).

I know Instagram and Facebook tell us that the "other" mom has it all together. I'm sorry, but has anyone tried to put shoes on a preschooler as you're hurrying out the door, while they scream, "I can do it," making you late? *Again!* Have you ever been annoyed at the clothes selected by your middle schooler or the things they gravitate to in their high school years? Isn't that a reflection on you? Disappointment as a mom can grind us to a halt if we allow it to define us instead of letting our identity in Christ define us.

Momma, listen—you're not a failure or the "late mom" or the "scatter-brained mom" or the "I'll bring paper plates" mom. God's love for you and your worth to him have nothing to do with whether or not your son called you last week, if you fed your family Chick-fil-A twice this week, or if dishes remain in your sink and laundry on your bed. And I'm so grateful!

In the words of my sweet husband, just keep going! Focus on the Father's love and grace to you and look for what he has for you next.

As the Lord reminded Israel in Isaiah, "Forget the former things; do not dwell on the past. See, I am doing a new thing! Now it springs up; do you not perceive it? I am making a way in the wilderness and streams in the wasteland" (Isaiah 43:18–19).

That day in the design building, God reminded me that my inability to draw had nothing to do with his love for me. Maybe it was my professor's method. Or maybe I would never need the ability to sketch paper bags thrown in a pile to be a designer. Or maybe my ability to draw just didn't matter to the direction the Father would take my life (at least not yet). I obviously didn't believe this in my failure and disappointment through the years. But that day, in that design studio, God redeemed my hurt simply and beautifully.

And he does the same for you.

So forget about the bread you forgot in the oven last night or your child's epic meltdown in Target yesterday. Your success as a mom is not measured by whether your children behave at the appropriate time, do well in math, or read their Bible on their own. God sees you as his beloved child, whom he loved enough to send Jesus to die in your place. He wants you to know you are his greatest joy … whether you can draw or not.

Reflecting on God's Faithfulness

Faithful Before: Can you look back and see where God has walked with you in a season of disappointment? Write about it here, thanking him for his goodness.

_____

_____

_____

_____

His Word: Read Ephesians 1:1–14. Did you notice how Paul encouraged the church at Ephesus with the blessings of Christ for the child of God? Fill in the chart below with the blessings for the child of God Paul describes:

Faithful Again: Are you currently struggling with a recent disappointment? Write out a prayer thanking God for walking with you before and asking him to remind you of his presence now.

_____

_____

_____

_____

#faithfulbeforefaithfulagain   DAY 6: Faithful in Disappointment

Day Seven

Present fears are less than horrible imaginings.

—William Shakespeare[9]

Day 7

Faithful in Fear

We were living in our first home south of Dallas, and I was *very* pregnant with our first child. Still feeling pretty good at this stage, I was enjoying every minute of it, minus the Texas heat. The third trimester in the Texas summer can be brutal!

My sister-in-law and her husband were moving to the Dallas area, and I had spent the day driving around town with them checking out apartments. As we pulled down our street at the end of the day, I noticed multiple police cars at our house. My husband approached me as I got out of the car. In his typical calm fashion, he told me, "It looks like we had a visitor today."

I know this makes zero sense, but for some reason, I immediately thought there was a mouse in the house. I mean, to me, *that* would be a most unwanted visitor. We'll call it pregnancy brain, but context clues were not my friend that day. He proceeded to explain we had been broken into, straight through the front door in broad daylight. They had taken jewelry, a video camera (you know the big black box, had-to-be-supported-on-your-shoulder model), and a few other minor things. Having only been married three years, we did not own a lot for this intruder—who had no obvious respect for private property—to snag.

I rubbed my wedding ring with my thumb, thankful I had worn it that day. If you've been pregnant in the summer, any season really, you know the appendage swelling that occurs. Unfortunately, that day I had not been wearing a ring my parents gave me for graduation. It had a ruby in the center and was surrounded by diamonds on all sides, reminiscent of the eye of a hurricane. The thought of never seeing that gift again was a sad blow. But the even more distressing outcome of that day's invasion was the mounting fear of it happening again. Fear soon became an ugly trap.

A few years later the alarm went off one night while we were sleeping. To say I panicked is an understatement. I ran into our closet and yelled for my husband to get the kids! I didn't even go and get my own children! Apparently, self-preservation in the height of fear supersedes motherly instincts. The door chime continued to go off every few seconds, as if someone came in and then left again. I literally could not breathe. Reggie quickly figured out that it was a glitch in the electrical system (later finding there was a staple through a wire). But by then, my heart was terrified and that revelation was mute.

I was scared. Again.

During the next few years, Reggie traveled a lot, leaving me home alone with our two daughters during the work week. My fear and anxiety didn't get any better for the many years that followed. I would call Reggie in the middle of the night, knowing he was thousands of miles away working and could do nothing about my fears. I often took the girls to stay with my parents, or my mom would stay with us. When we later moved into a new home, all of the tiles in our foyer and kitchen popped loose overnight. It sounded like gunfire. (Look it up, gunfire is exactly what it sounds like.) I had a neighbor come spend the night, as Reg was on the road.

I knew this fear gripping my heart was based on past events, but it was also starting to affect different areas of current and future realities. But what could I do about it?

I had studied my Bible for years and knew what Scripture said about fear and courage and God's presence. But I still often thought, *Can it really be that easy?* I feared not just another home invasion. Fears surfaced when I would encounter something new, thought about my children's future and my responsibilities to them, or even ventured somewhere alone. *What if I don't know what to do? What if something goes wrong? Why, yes, I do love the ocean, but um, no, I am not going snorkeling!*

> Have I not commanded you? Be strong and courageous. Do not be afraid; do not be discouraged, for the LORD your God will be with you wherever you go. (Joshua 1:9)

This Old Testament verse comes at the beginning of the book of Joshua and shows up right after Moses died. Joshua, a leader in the making, had been with Moses for years, learning from God's chosen deliverer to lead the children of Israel into the promised land. With Moses now gone, it was up to Joshua to continue in his place and finish what Moses had started.

What an assignment! I would bet a potato chip (as my childhood pastor used to say) that such a monumental task would instill some semblance of doubt in anyone's abilities. But God knew his heart and reminded Joshua he would be with him and he did not need to be afraid. Joshua had plenty to look back on, reflecting on the times God had done what he said he would and fought for them on their journey thus far. Always faithful to his word, God would lead them to the "land flowing with milk and honey" (Exodus 3:8).

Thoughts of doubt and fear have taken up residence in my mind much differently in the later years. There is another Scripture in the New Testament that bolsters my confidence in Christ and guides me in those times when fear rears its ugly head and threatens to lead me in a spiraling thought process. I love how the New International Version of this verse describes taking these thoughts captive as they attempt to push God's power over the world out of the picture.

> For though we live in the world, we do not wage war as the world does. The weapons we fight with are not the weapons of the world. On the contrary, they have divine power to demolish strongholds. We demolish arguments and every pretension that sets itself up against the knowledge of God, and we take captive every thought to make it obedient to Christ. (2 Corinthians 10:3–5)

I'm still learning to recognize my own thought processes, becoming more familiar with God's voice with each passing day. Acknowledging the loud, overbearing doubts that the Enemy throws at me has been huge. I have discovered that asking myself where those thoughts come from and remembering the truth of Scripture is key to finding freedom. "For the Spirit God gave us does not make us timid, but gives us power, love and self-discipline" (2 Timothy 1:7).

Amid the fun, rewarding, joyful life we live as Christians, we will still encounter hard things, unexpected "visitors" that threaten to steal our joy and hold us hostage to our fears. But God has promised to be with us and never leave us. We can have courage in knowing he wins each battle. Every time.

> I will give you every place where you set your foot, as I promised Moses.... No one will be able to stand against you all the days of your life. As I was with Moses, so I will be with you; I will never leave you nor forsake you. Be strong and courageous, because you will lead these people to inherit the land I swore to their ancestors to give them. (Joshua 1:3, 5–6)

Reflecting on God's Faithfulness

Faithful Before: Can you look back and see where God has walked with you through a season of fear? Write out your experience here.

_____
_____
_____
_____

His Word: Write Joshua 1:9 in your own words.

_____
_____
_____
_____

Faithful Again: Is there a current fear you are struggling with? Write a prayer, asking God to remind you of his presence now, and thank him for his work in your past fears.

_____
_____
_____
_____

#faithfulbeforefaithfulagain

Day Eight

Nothing on the outside compares to Thy presence on my inside.

—A. W. Tozer[10]

Day 8

Faithful in Presence

We keep staples in our kitchen—spices, oils, flour, and sugars—so they're ready at a moment's notice when we need to finish various dishes throughout the week. The assembling of just the right ingredients creates a yummy dish that otherwise could not stand alone. Just the right amount of this, and a pinch of that, close by when its use is warranted. This is fine in the kitchen. But we often do this in relationships as well. We search for that "perfect" mate. Someone with all the "right" qualities who will complete us and complement our personality. Someone we can turn to 24/7. Someone who understands us.

But the older we get, the more we realize not one person on the planet fully understands, agrees, or sees our side of things every single time—just like no one ingredient in our pantry works in epicurean harmony with all recipes.

I love my husband dearly. We dated for three and a half years, and, at the time of this writing, we have been married for thirty-four years. And as fantastic as he is, he does not understand female experiences. He doesn't know the discomfort of menstrual cramps, the feeling of carrying a baby for nine months, the pain of a contraction, or the experience of birthing a child. He is not as emotionally driven as I tend to be, and thankfully brings the calm, rational wisdom I often lack.

So I confide in girlfriends for those conversations he simply cannot grasp—postmenopausal weight gain, the worries only a mom can understand, the emotions we go through with our kids. But my friends don't necessarily understand my work life. So I have another set of friends I can relate to about work. You get the idea.

It can feel lonely when we realize that not one person in the world understands us completely or is accessible to us at a given time.

And nobody wants to feel alone.

After I graduated from high school, my father requested I take a couple of summer classes at the Bible college where he was the dean of students. So the summer before I went away to college, I took Old Testament and New Testament survey classes, a broad sweep of basic doctrine and an overview of these two sections of the Bible. Among many things, we studied several words that refer to God's character.

Omniscient describes God as all-knowing.

Omnipotent describes God as all-powerful.

Omnipresent describes God as always present, everywhere, all the time.

I'll never forget writing those words and definitions on white index cards with blue lines to memorize for the upcoming test. These new concepts were difficult to grasp at first, but they brought comfort through the years as I found God's wisdom, strength, and presence in my own life, examples of how a simple vocabulary worked in real life.

An article by *The Gospel Coalition* on God's omnipresence describes this portion of his character like this:

> He is with us, not to destroy us, but to forgive and to save us from sin. So this "with you," this redeeming divine presence, is found often in Scripture as his gracious promise. To Isaac, God said, "I will be with you and will bless you" (Genesis 26:3) and that language often forms the basis of God's redemptive covenant.... It should not surprise us that a biblical name for Jesus is Immanuel, God with us. (Isaiah 7:14; Matthew 1:23)[11]

God is with us.

When pumping in the middle of the night, crying from exhaustion in your closet to keep from waking your husband, he is there.

When holding a hot, sick baby while praying for the medicine to break the fever, he is there.

While waiting for the second blue line to appear, after it hasn't changed in several months, he is there.

When crying from dropping off your oldest on her first day of kindergarten in a new town, he is there.

When you wish you could talk to your mother-in-law one more time, if only to apologize, he is there.

When you rush to the sink to wash the blood off your hands, wondering if you could have done something different to keep from miscarrying, he is there.

When you watch your children learn life's lessons the hard way, he is there.

When your firstborn goes to college and moves hours from home, he is there.

When your to-do list appears unmanageable, he is there.

When you move your last child to college and return to an empty house for the first time since before becoming a mother, he is there.

When you cry as you sweep freshly shaven hair off the floor as a result of your mom's chemo treatments, he is there.

When you wish someone understood, he is there.

God's presence brings comfort, direction, and protection. As the children of Israel were led by Moses out of slavery in Egypt, God led them in a pillar of a cloud and a pillar of fire to guide them day and night. They could follow his presence in the cloud, which provided instruction for them to stop or go as he willed. "Neither the pillar of cloud by day nor the pillar of fire by night left its place in front of the people" (Exodus 13:22).

Later, once the Israelites had built the tabernacle, the glory of the Lord entered this house of worship, filling it with the cloud and resting there. "So the cloud of the Lord was over the tabernacle by day, and fire was in the cloud by night, in the sight of all the Israelites during all their travels" (Exodus 40:38).

In his first letter to the Corinthians, Paul explains where God's presence resides through the Holy Spirit. He refers to our bodies as the "temple of God," where God's presence now dwells in the heart of the Christ follower. "Don't you know that you yourselves are God's temple and that God's Spirit dwells in your midst?" (1 Corinthians 3:16).

The Holy Spirit's presence in the heart of the believer provides the same guidance as the cloud. He is the Comforter, not by sight but by faith, now residing in our hearts. God makes his dwelling (John 1:14) with us in a new way, providing an ever-present existence in the lives of those who call him Lord. There is peace is the presence of God.

Reflecting on God's Faithfulness

Faithful Before: Can you look back and see a time when God's presence was a clear comfort to you? Write about it here, thanking him for his goodness.

_____

_____

_____

_____

His Word: Read Exodus 33:7–11, which describes the *tent of meeting,* before God instructed the building of the tabernacle, where they met with God. Then read John 14:16–17. What do you learn about God's presence?

_____

_____

_____

_____

Faithful Again: Are you currently longing for God's presence? Write out a prayer thanking God for walking with you before and asking him to remind you of his presence now.

_____

_____

_____

_____

Day Nine

Some people believe holding on and hanging in there are signs of great strength. However, there are times when it takes much more strength to know when to let go and then do it.

—Ann Landers[12]

Day 9

Faithful in Identity

It was like a slow roll from yellow to red. We had two more years with kids in school before they all left the nest. Twelve years of grade school sounds like a lifetime when looking at a squishy newborn. But my twenty-five years with three children at home was soon coming to an end. My influence, time, and space with my three children were shifting.

And I wasn't a fan.

I was a stay-at-home mom for sixteen years before returning to the workforce when my oldest hit junior year. A career was simply never my jam. Even though I didn't love working and had no ambition of climbing any ladder, I loved the reason I took the job: to help with the upcoming twelve-year budgetary line item of college tuition. Dividing my time between home and work was difficult at best, a tug-of-war of sorts. In retrospect, maybe God used it as a weaning period so I wouldn't have to adjust from full-time stay-at-home mom to no longer having kiddos at home. He knew what was ahead for my heart, even if I didn't fully understand.

The reality of my situation hit me the year my youngest was to graduate from high school. Looking back, those couple of years were some of the hardest in my life. (If you worked with me then, I apologize.) His graduation pictures were taken at a small community park where he played his first baseball game as an elementary student. One of my favorite photos became my desktop screen saver at work, inducing a self-inflicted sadness for the duration of the school year.

Why did I torture myself?

It wasn't that my baby was graduating. It wasn't even that all three of my kids were grown. For the first time in years, I was faced with the question: *What now?* Was I now considered off duty after twenty-five years? I suddenly felt unneeded. The slow realization of where my identity had settled turned into a heavy cloud that shadowed many of the coming days.

I had prayerfully done my job as a mom to the best of my abilities. They had all three grown into independent, self-reliant, hardworking, and fun-to-be-around young adults who love each other dearly. (Check out episode 35 about empty nesting from the *Drive Thru Moms* podcast for an inside peek.)

Did my role as carpool organizer and meal planner usurp my title as a child of the King? Were medals of honor given for completing long lists of errands, cleaning house, doing endless loads of laundry, and chauffeuring kids to countless activities and practices? Did these roles and tasks validate my position and title of *mom*?

In my search and conversations with the Lord about what was next, I ventured into a new job and later into podcasting in 2020. But amid COVID shutdowns and a desire to share more of God's goodness, I reeled in my widespread activities in the spring of 2021 and narrowed my focus. I needed to slow it down and find more time for him in my day, truly putting him first for the first time in a long time. He clearly had more for me to do. I was needed elsewhere.

So I listened. I paused recording for the *Drive Thru Moms* podcast and focused on studying, reading, and prioritizing God. This time with him fulfilled me in a way I really cannot describe. But more than that, it reminded me of my favorite role … I was a child of God first.

> But to all who did receive him, who believed in his name, he gave the right to become children of God. (John 1:12 ESV)

I don't know if you've ever seen the TV series *The Chosen*, but it's a moving depiction of Christ, his ministry, his disciples, and other players of that day. The writers use creative license in many scenes, filling in the details Scripture doesn't include.

My favorite episode is season two, episode three, because it shares a conversation moms across the globe can relate to. In one of those fictional scenes, Mary, the mother of Jesus, sits around a campfire with the disciples and shares how her title of mom of Jesus had changed. She is no longer needed as a nurturer or caregiver. She knew Jesus really didn't need her, especially as the Son of God, at least not like other children. She wasn't belligerent or mad about that, and she didn't even complain. She was just a loving mom, reveling in the stories of Jesus's childhood—a mom who missed the simpler times of his youth.

By the end of Mary and the disciples' campfire conversation, Jesus returns to the scene and heads to his tent. After a long day of ministering, healing, praying, and listening to people, he is visibly exhausted. Mary, in true mom fashion, sees his weariness and immediately appears at his side to help him prepare for bed. She assists him as he removes his sandals, and she washes his feet.[13]

He still didn't need her in the same way he had as a child, but her present opportunity found her in a new role. Even the mother of Jesus could miss her son and days gone by, regardless of knowing the vital ministry ahead of him. But God added a new unexpected line item to her résumé as mom … servant.

I sobbed.

The more I realized my identity had become deeply entrenched in the lives of my family, perhaps even to the detriment of my own spiritual growth and sanctification, the more God spoke the truth of who I really am … a servant of the Most High King.

And unlike the once-growing, mess-making, ever-eating kiddos of my young mothering years, my identity as his child would never change. I am more than a mom, chauffeur, brownie maker, school committee member, wannabe chef, domestic engineer, and a new fave, nana. My identity is more than the roles I play. My identity is more than the titles I have held in the past or the ones I currently answer to. My identity is in the love and forgiveness I possess, due to the sacrificial life given for me.

Do I still miss my kids living at home at times? You know it! But being in God's presence daily helps heal and soothe my heart, elevating my title of *mom* to *daughter* and *child of God*. "See what great love the Father has lavished on us, that we should be called children of God! And that is what we are!" (1 John 3:1).

Reflecting on God's Faithfulness

Faithful Before: Can you look back and see how God has walked with you through the multiple roles you play as a mom? Write about it here, thanking him for his goodness.

_____
_____
_____
_____

His Word: Write out the ways Psalm 145:14–20 describes the Lord's care for our mom hearts.

_____
_____
_____
_____

Faithful Again: Are you currently giving your identity as mom more value than being a child of God? Write out a prayer asking him to remind you of your most important role as his daughter.

_____
_____
_____
_____

#faithfulbeforefaithfulagain   DAY 9: Faithful in Identity

Day Ten

Safety comes in our nearness to God, not in our distance from our enemies.

—Dillon Burroughs[14]

Day 10

Faithful in Protection

Weekend lounging was an anomaly back in our early parenting days. Those weekend mornings were usually spent at gymnastics meets, soccer fields, basketball courts, or baseball fields. Rare free weekends were often spent on quick road trips south of town to see the grandparents. My husband and I often tag teamed drop-offs, game watching, and pickups so we could spread our time between our three love bugs.

One particular Saturday was free of commitments, and we were thrilled with a much-needed day at home. We were busy cleaning, washing laundry, mowing, and other tedious yet necessary chores. Well, apparently not all of us. As Reggie and I chatted in his office about what chore was next on our list, our three-year-old preschooler rushed in full of excitement, sans shirt or pants. Dressed only in his tighty-whities, he shouted about his latest adventure.

"That was awesome!" he yelled, as he ran into the office.

"What was awesome?" I asked naively. I later wished I could have retracted my question. Some things my heart could live without knowing!

"I just came down the laundry chute! It was so much fun! I'm going to do it again!"

Once we picked our jaws up off the floor, we burst the excited bubble of the adorable, blue-eyed preschooler standing before us. Much to his disappointment, we told this half-naked explorer in unison, "No, you will *not* do that again!"

When we had built our house in 1997, I discovered that the third bedroom upstairs, empty at the time, sat directly above the laundry room. We asked the builders if it was possible to move the laundry room cabinets directly under the empty section in the framing, making it possible to add a laundry chute from the bedroom closet. When any laundry was dropped into the chute, it landed in the cabinets right below. It was genius, if I do say so myself. Instead of gathering up all our dirty clothes, I only had to walk to the washer and dryer and open the cabinet doors. (I say it's for dirty clothes, unless you're a seven-year-old who doesn't fancy putting clean clothes away. In that case, you just drop the folded clean clothes back into the laundry chute, thinking no one is the wiser.)

Initially, we did not tell our middle child about the laundry chute, for fear she would do exactly what the baby of the family decided to do that day. After the initial shock of our son's announcement, my husband and I immediately ran to the laundry room and looked up into the framed-in passageway. I'm still not sure why we felt the need to go to the scene of the crime, rummaging through the mounds of dirty clothes our children had dropped that week. What was done was done, and he obviously was no worse for the wear. He was so ecstatic we could practically see those little wheels spinning in his head, planning another trip. But we took a flashlight and looked into the chute. To our horror and shock, we saw multiple nails of considerable length exposed up and down the sheetrock. They stuck out like empty branches on a tree in winter. It was a sheer miracle that our precious baby boy had not one scratch on him.

Nothing.

What if he had tried to stand up when he landed? How in the world was he all in one piece without a visible aftereffect to mark his exploit? I'm not clear on how you can be thankful, utterly amazed, and sick to your stomach at the same time. But you can.

To this day, this story still makes my stomach queasy, and it's been about twenty years. What was intended to be a shortcut for this stay-at-home mom instantly became a source of regret. I would now worry about potential injury and future escapades.

After I stopped crying and squeezing the stuffing out of our son in relief, we instructed him to never go down the laundry chute again. But let's be honest, he was three. We knew the temptation of the repeated thrill would remain a draw since the chute resided right in his bedroom closet. Much to his chagrin, we then kept a nailed board across the opening and temporarily eliminated access until he was old enough to use it properly (or to be honest, too big to go down it).

I should have seen it coming though. There were red flags that some little, problem-solving, adventure-seeking, three-year-old boy just couldn't leave alone. Occasionally, when

I opened the cabinet doors and pulled out dirty clothes the kids had put in, I would find a toy, block, or ball. Somebody was testing the waters, and I had missed it.

But in all of the "what ifs" and "don't ever do that agains," God reminded me of his protection. Again. The Father in heaven, aware of our nature, curiosities, and sinful hearts, unbeknownst to us, steps in and lovingly covers us and protects us from harm. And we can find joy and comfort in his protection. "But let all who take refuge in you be glad; let them ever sing for joy. Spread your protection over them, that those who love your name may rejoice in you" (Psalm 5:11).

How many times have we been spared injury or trauma or just plain hurt because someone prayed for our protection? How many angels have been around us, waiting in the wings just in case they were needed, standing guard, and waiting for a nod of direction from the Lord? As parents, prayer plays such a huge role in the lives of our children. We pray for their physical, mental, and spiritual protection from things that draw them away from their relationship with God. "If you say, 'The Lord is my refuge,' and you make the Most High your dwelling, no harm will overtake you, no disaster will come near your tent. For he will command his angels concerning you to guard you in all your ways" (Psalm 91:9–11).

I can't wait to get to heaven, for a lot of reasons. But for one, I bet the angels will have the best stories.

Reflecting on God's Faithfulness

Faithful Before: Can you look back and see God's protection of you or someone you love? Write about it here, thanking him for his goodness.

_____
_____
_____
_____

His Word: Read Psalm 138:7 and Psalm 16:1, then write out one of them below.

_____
_____
_____
_____

Faithful Again: How does Psalm 18:16–19 describe God's protection?

_____
_____
_____
_____

Day Eleven

God is more interested in our response than He is in the tangible results.

—*Elisabeth Elliot*[15]

Day 11

Faithful in Conviction

We started empty nesting with a bang, taking advantage of the real estate market's high prices and selling our home of twenty-four years. The sale of our home allowed us to fund some exciting opportunities. One perk was finding a rental a few minutes from my parents, who are both in their eighties, so we could spend more time with them.

When I stopped by to check in one day, my dad handed me an article he had cut from the paper. Clipping newspaper articles has been his approach as long as I can remember, even in today's world of copying and pasting links to send via text or email. The newspaper article referred to recent flooding in Kentucky near his hometown. I had already heard about it and brushed it off. "Yeah, I saw it," I replied. He turned around with the article in hand and walked back to the living room.

Mindlessly surfing Facebook that night while we watched TV, I saw that my cousin, who lives in Kentucky, had posted a picture of my grandparents. The post shared a story passed down through our family. It was the same story my dad had tried to remind me of earlier that day. When my father was a child, two storms flooded the tiny hillside village where he grew up. Rising waters had lifted the piano, only to drop it in a different spot in their living room and land it on its side. The piano stuck in the sludge and muddy residue and required crowbars to loosen and set it in its original upright position. The water rose so high it left stains mere inches from the ceiling in my dad's living room—a permanent reminder of the water's devastation. His home flooded twice as a child, leaving indelible marks on a young boy.

My dismissal of him earlier that day pricked my heart. The recent flooding had triggered painful memories from my father's childhood. The article he had tried to show me explained that over thirty people had died as a result of the recent floods. Clearly still troubled all these years later, in typical fashion these days, my father had asked, "Have I told you about the floods and how the piano got stuck?" He was empathizing with the families. He knew how it felt to be afraid of rising waters, since he too had lived it as a child. His grief and cautious approach suddenly made much more sense to me.

And I had totally dismissed him. But why? Was I really that callous that I didn't care about his feelings? Or was I not ready to accept my aging father's new reality? Instead of listening to my intelligent, multi-degreed, former dean of students, teacher, and preacher dad struggle to share a story, I said, "Uh huh." I ignored him rather than choosing to listen to him. I had protected myself instead of indulging my sweet, elderly father with a huge heart for others, despite the memory issues that plagued him.

My tears of conviction led me to do something that's becoming a lost art. I apologized. I had to pick up my mom the next day to run an errand, but I first stopped in and talked to Daddy to apologize for my dismissal of our conversation. The story of the recent flooding had obviously affected him deeply, but in his mercy, grace, and love as a father, he forgave me for brushing him off and said he loved me.

How often do we let the Father in heaven convict our hearts of some action or inaction or some harsh words we've uttered? Do we recognize his conviction? But more than that, do we act on it? Understanding the need to forgive and to ask for forgiveness of others starts with recognizing the forgiveness we receive from God, which we truly don't deserve. We are all guilty of sin (Romans 3:23). As believers, when we miss the mark of living a Christlike life, it requires rectifying our missteps with a friend, coworker, or loved one.

> Therefore, if you are offering your gift at the altar and there remember that your brother or sister has something against you, leave your gift there in front of the altar. First, go and be reconciled to them; then come and offer your gift. (Matthew 5:23–24)

As mothers, it's easy to see when our children are rude to a sibling or unkind to a friend. We admonish them to apologize, make amends, and obey our requests without an argument. The truth is, we also often miss the mark, but for some reason, we don't see it in ourselves. Even if we do, do we have someone in our sphere of friends to hold us accountable? We don't typically have our mom following us around, pointing out our mistakes, short tempers, or inappropriate actions. And to be honest, would we flag such comments as judgmental or hypocritical? I mean, they do it too! Right?

But even a man after God's own heart needed accountability. As the king of Israel, David slept with Bathsheba, the wife of another man. To hide his sin, David ordered her husband to the front battle lines, sending the man to his death. Once her husband was out of the way, David then brought Bathsheba into his home to be his wife. He was the king, after all. He could do what he wanted, right? But the Lord sent the prophet Nathan to put David in his place. Nathan shared another man's story of sinful actions, similar to David's. David rebuked the man in the hypothetical story, saying this man must die. But Nathan informed him, "You are the man" (2 Samuel 12:7).

Convicted of his sin, David cried out for forgiveness, and Scripture says the Lord forgave him. Yet his sin was not without consequence. Bathsheba became pregnant, and the child did not survive. Nonetheless, David rose from his grief, cleaned himself up, and worshipped the Lord (2 Samuel 12:20).

Motherhood is sanctifying work. As Christ followers, when we see our sin, we must maintain a soft heart that recognizes the voice of the Holy Spirit and acts according to Scripture. God sometimes painfully prunes and trims the pieces of our lives that impede our growth. But faithful friends who nudge us back to living with a pure heart bring us into closer fellowship with the Father.

And that's what I want.

Reflecting on God's Faithfulness

Faithful Before: Do you remember a season where conviction from God was clear? Write a prayer, thanking him for prompting you to restore what was broken.

_____
_____
_____
_____

His Word: Read the prayer from David in Psalm 51 and let the Lord speak to you. Write what he reveals to your heart.

_____
_____
_____
_____

Faithful Again: What is the Holy Spirt currently convicting you of? Write a prayer asking God to give you clarity and boldness in your next steps.

_____
_____
_____
_____

#faithfulbeforefaithfulagain

Day Twelve

Walking with a friend in the dark is better than walking alone in the light.

—Helen Keller[16]

Day 12

Faithful in Friendship

My mother was diagnosed with breast cancer several years ago, in the fall before my oldest daughter got married. I would not wish that experience on anyone. It is heart-wrenching to watch someone you love go through sickness, pain, and physical changes while learning to adapt to a new normal.

As a young mother, I had spent several days a week while my girls were in school staying with my grandmother in the hospital. She suffered a short battle with ovarian cancer. Watching my grandmother slip away and into the arms of Jesus was difficult, to be sure. But witnessing my mother and her sister lose their mother ushered in a reality I was not ready for.

Thankfully, my mother's treatment went well and she survived. Once chemo and radiation ended and her wigs were tucked back in their box, we thanked God for her complete healing and his presence in the middle of it all. We prayed her cancer would not rear its ugly head again.

A few years later, during my mom's routine yearly check-up and scan, the oncologist discovered a concerning spot. It felt like just yesterday when we had swept up her freshly shaven hair off the bathroom floor. I was a mess at the prospect of witnessing her go through it again and at the potential of losing her. I texted my BFF the latest news, asking if she would pray for my mother. The willingness of an available friend is a gift to the one in distress. I then told her I was headed out to take a walk.

I walked and prayed anxiously along a busy, tree-lined street near our neighborhood. As I breathed in the fresh air to alleviate my fears, I looked up and saw my friend coming toward me from the opposite direction. She took my hand and turned to join my route, falling in step and walking beside me. She didn't talk or ask me questions. She just let me cry. She held my hand and walked silently with me down a road that suddenly seemed all too far to walk alone.

She was simply there.

In the Bible, Job is a just, righteous, and highly respected man. God had blessed him with incredible wealth, family, and honor. But in the second chapter of Job, God allows Satan to test him in various ways, causing Job to lose his possessions, family, servants, and more. That's a lot of loss! And yet, Job chose to praise God.

Unfortunately for Job, it got worse. Satan asked God for permission to pursue Job further, and God allowed him to "touch" Job with a physical illness, only sparing his life. Despite his ailment, pain, and sorrow, Job never placed blame at God's feet (Job 1:22; 2:10). Job longed for healing; his wife even prompted him to "curse God and die!" (Job 2:9). And yet, God said, "Job did not sin in what he said" (Job 2:10).

Enter his friends, over the horizon, showing up in the hour of need—at just the right time.

> When Job's three friends, Eliphaz the Temanite, Bildad the Shuhite and Zophar the Naamathite, heard about all the troubles that had come upon him, they set out from their homes and met together by agreement to go and sympathize with him and comfort him. (Job 2:11)

Three of Job's friends heard of his situation and traveled to be at his side. For the first part of their time together, the friends let him talk. For seven days and nights, they said nothing. Can you think of *one* woman who would sit and be silent for an entire week? Job cried out, complained, and dumped his problems on them. He flushed his heart and mind clean through his soulful expression. They just listened.

> When they saw him from a distance they could hardly recognize him; they began to weep aloud, and they tore their robes and sprinkled dust on their heads. Then they sat on the ground with him for seven days and seven nights. No one said a word to him, because they saw how great his suffering was. (Job 2:12–13)

Faithful before Faithful again

Friendship doesn't always mean sharing advice, words of wisdom, or even comic relief. To be fair, Job's friends didn't end up with stellar words for him. God condemned them in the last chapter of the book for not speaking truth about him to their friend in his darkest hour. Maybe they should have followed my friend's example!

But to me, the best part of this story is that Job prayed for them. And because of his petition, God accepted his prayer. His actions as a friend to them resulted in their restoration. The Lord also blessed Job with "twice as much as he had before" (Job 42:10). Even family and friends who had known him previous to his despair came to comfort him.

The simple presence of a friend to come alongside, hold hands, cry together, and speak wise words displays the heart of the Father—a heart of pure and selfless love. True selfless friendship reveals the Father in heaven, as if to say, "I'm physically here in the flesh, through your friend, showing my love in their actions."

That hug, squeeze of a hand, or act of kindness is loaded with God's purpose and love for us. "Your love, Lord, reaches to the heavens, your faithfulness to the skies.... How priceless is your unfailing love, O God! People take refuge in the shadow of your wings" (Psalm 36:5, 7).

God's provision of friendship in our times of need is one of life's greatest gifts. David had Nathan, Paul had Timothy, and Jesus had the disciples. "I no longer call you servants, because a servant does not know his master's business. Instead I have called you friends, for everything that I learned from my Father I have made known to you" (John 15:15).

As believers in Christ, we always have him at our side. He walks beside us, present in the troubles we face, a friend always waiting for us to take his hand. "One who has unreliable friends soon comes to ruin, but there is a friend who sticks closer than a brother" (Proverbs 18:24).

Reflecting on God's Faithfulness

Faithful Before: Can you look back and see a friend God has provided to walk with you through a particular season? Write about it here, thanking him for his provision.

_____

_____

_____

_____

His Word: Write out the action words used to describe the appropriate ways Job's friends responded in Job 2:11–13. Then write down the Lord's charge against them in Job 42:7–9. What kind of friend does Scripture call us to be?

_____

_____

_____

_____

Faithful Again: Are you currently in need of a friend? Or are you not sure how to be a friend to someone God has placed in your life? Write out a prayer asking God for his provision of a godly friendship.

_____

_____

_____

_____

#faithfulbeforefaithfulagain

Day Thirteen

The key is not to prioritize what's on your schedule, but to schedule your priorities.

—Stephen Covey[17]

Day 13

Faithful in Priorities

With a few gift cards in hand, I ventured out to take advantage of the Fourth of July Independence Day sales. America's birthday! I expected a sea of red, white, and blue decor, along with sales tags galore. I pulled up to the first stop, hopeful to see how far this gift card would take me. Having spent a few years working retail, and with decades of shopping under my belt, I made a beeline for the back of the store in search of the sale rack and bargain bin.

Once at the back wall, I noticed a waist-high bookshelf behind a display. You could only see it if you walked all the way around it and made a one-eighty, fully turning around. Then and *only* then could you see what was on the small shelf and in the tiny galvanized bucket resting next to it on the floor. Much to my dismay, on this day of America's celebration, only three or four American flag placemats rested on the shelf and one flag-stitched throw pillow sat in the bucket on the floor. I had found the bargain bin.

I then realized no other Fourth of July sale signs, flags, or decorations were hung anywhere in the store. I walked back up to the front, perusing the landscape of the retail space to confirm my suspicion. These items in the far back corner of the store were the only evidence of one of the biggest holidays in our country.

My mom is a former high school American history teacher. She can spot a flag a mile away. Our family dearly loves the United States, flaws and all. To say I was appalled is a fair statement. How in the world could you have one of the biggest holidays of the year not reflected in your merchandise? Even strictly from an opportunity to move summer merchandise, the Fourth generally kicks off that season of clearance, and they were missing it. I was baffled and felt a rising compulsion to complain.

The phrase "Nobody puts Baby in a corner!" rang through my disillusioned mind. (That's a *Dirty Dancing* movie reference for you young ones.) But as I walked toward the checkout desk to speak to the manager, mulling over how to carefully share my indignation, the Holy Spirit tapped me on the shoulder.

Just like that, out of the blue, a thought came out of nowhere! *Wait, Lord! Can we get back to the offense at hand? This store's priorities aren't about me. Are you saying I have moved something to the bottom back corner shelf in my life?*

This was about more than patriotism. Griping at a sales clerk was not the point. If I'm honest, I'm not sure my outrage would have depicted Christ at all. Taking a deep breath and changing my direction, I walked past the register and out to my car.

Okay, Lord, what did that have to do with me? How did today's missed opportunity to show allegiance mirror my heart? God's use of an ordinary moment prompted a look at my own priorities before I threw that stone. The moment was beautiful, if only to me, as a mom charged with living out godly priorities to those around me. It was also for the good of my own heart. Was God first in my life? Did my actions reflect a heart surrendered to God first and above all?

As Christians, we can be called judgmental at best and hypocrites at worst. Our walk reflects our priorities. Do I spend time with God to complete the daily to-do list or to learn more about his character? Am I living out what I preach to the children in my life, making him truly first? What I live in front of them is important. Or am I placing him on a small back shelf, where no one can really see, but available in case someone asks?

In the book of Revelation, John is tasked with writing letters to seven churches based on his vision. In his first letter, he writes to the church in Ephesus. At first, he praises them for their hard work and perseverance, then challenges them. "Yet I hold this against you: You have forsaken the love you had at first. Consider how far you have fallen! Repent and do the things you did at first" (Revelation 2:4–5).

Overcommitted seasons of life can derail us from spiritual growth when we put those commitments, work, or even family ahead of our time devoted to deepening our relationship with God. After an unmemorable drive home, I wrestled with the Lord about my morning, asking him to search my heart. "Search me, God, and know my heart; test me and know my anxious thoughts. See if there is any offensive way in me, and lead me in the way everlasting" (Psalm 139:23–24).

He's always good to oblige, and he provided me clarity and uncomfortable reminders with verses I've tucked away for safekeeping for such an occasion. For the last year and a half, he had faithfully reminded me to stay on the path he had called me to—slow down, pause, and put him first.

Overcommitment isn't intentional. It sometimes happens in an unconscious effort to keep up with the pace of modern life. But being too busy can be an effective tactic of the Enemy in the life of every Christian. A classroom mom commitment here, a PTA meeting there, it all adds up. Add your kids' practice and game schedules, your work responsibilities, and throw in social media, and your schedule is more than full. The never-ending list of typical mom duties makes it hard to prioritize spending time doing much of anything else. None of our mom commitments or other responsibilities are bad, but anything that squeezes out available time to deepen our relationship with Christ is idolatry. Before we know it, God is pushed lower on the list in our planner and eventually relinquished to a spot on the bottom shelf. God's desire for us is to know him fully and more intimately. And that takes time, commitment, and discipline.

In part of the Sermon on the Mount, in Matthew 5 and 6, Jesus reminds his audience where their focus should be first and foremost. "But seek first his kingdom and his righteousness, and all these things will be given to you as well" (Matthew 6:33).

Having left the store in a tizzy, I knew just what to do with my yet-unused gift cards. I pulled up the store's website anyway. I placed my order, including four pillows and eight placemats, each adorned in the good ol' red, white, and blue. Those American flags will most definitely appear on my couches and table each July, thrilling the heart of my beloved American-history-teaching momma. But to me, their presence won't be a reminder of a store's failure to show their patriotism. Instead they will be a reflection of a priority the Holy Spirit whispered to my heart that day. There is only one first place, and it is reserved for the one and only heavenly Father.

Seek him first, momma. The rest will come.

Reflecting on God's Faithfulness

Faithful Before: Can you point to a time when you put the Lord first above the chaos in your life and saw him work? Write about it here, thanking him for his goodness during that season.

_____
_____
_____
_____

His Word: Read Matthew 6:33 and Isaiah 55:6–9. Write what God asks of us and the difference we find in focusing on him.

_____
_____
_____
_____

Faithful Again: Are you currently struggling with prioritizing your time with God? Write out a few steps you can take to dedicate time with him and remember the "love you had at first," spoken of in Revelation. He will meet you there.

_____
_____
_____
_____

#faithfulbeforefaithfulagain

Day Fourteen

All I have seen teaches me to trust the Creator for all I have not seen.

—Ralph Waldo Emerson[18]

Day 14

Faithful in Uncertainty

I live in Texas, where it rarely snows. We are more prone to get a layer of ice than snow when wintery weather blows in. I'm not adept at the meteorological implications. My husband is the weather tracker in the family. A winter weather alert normally brings only a light dusting of snow, disappointing schoolchildren across the metroplex. Anything more than that turns into a sloppy, wet slushfest on the roads, only to refreeze overnight. Once refrozen, it makes for treacherous treks to work, school, and other necessary travels.

When icy roads proved to be a deterrent to driving when I was a young adult, my dad would occasionally chauffeur me to work. I was a fresh college graduate with a new full-time job in downtown Dallas, but those were the days you went to work no matter what. Working remotely wasn't a thing yet. Northerners often remark that those of us in the South do not know how to navigate the roads in such weather.

They are not wrong.

My dad driving me to work downtown, some thirty miles from our home in the suburbs, protected me from potential harm. I was comforted knowing he had racked up many a mile driving in such conditions over the years. His driving résumé was impressive compared to mine, and I learned a lot when he was at the wheel, confident and in charge. He would share tips and tricks about how to follow the car ahead and how to steer if you began to slide. He reminded me to look for sand put out by the city to provide traction. The key was to look ahead and find the path prepared ahead of me.

Not that long ago, we had one such day. Just ice, no snow. It had been on the ground for a couple of days, so the ice had frozen, melted, been driven on, and refrozen. Lovely. But I had to make my icy journey solo, as an adult whose father was not driving.

What if I slide or get stuck?
What if I have a wreck?
Do I have a blanket in the car?
I hope my insurance card is up to date!

My natural instinct was to freeze and worry about the road ahead. But if I stopped long enough to gather my wits and take a deep breath, I could hear my father's voice speaking words of encouragement and direction. He reminded me to follow the icy ruts that had been created ahead of me. Their path would help me navigate the road. Those ruts of the previously traveled roads would provide traction, helping me stay on course and eliminating any unwanted off-road excursions.

Most people don't hear the audible voice of God speaking words of wisdom. But wouldn't that be awesome! I love those stories in Scripture when his voice can be audibly heard. For me, it's typically a whisper that pierces my heart—a realization and remembrance of God's Word that rings true in the moment. At that moment in the car, God took time to calm my anxious heart, drawing me to himself through reminders of his Word. In quiet moments when fear rears its ugly head, God speaks directly to my heart. He turns around my thought process that leads me to believe that whatever is in front of me is up to me and reminds me that it is not.

On that drive, I immediately heard the Lord whisper to my soul, "Lynn, I have laid things in front of you, paved the way, even sent people to you who have been through similar experiences to those you have been placed in. Trust me and follow the ruts."

It wasn't just about the icy road.

Let's face it, some seasons of life are more difficult than others. Some are short-lived, like trying to get your temper-tantruming two-year-old in the car or wrestling your middle schooler out of bed before they rack up another tardy. Other junctures last much longer, like months and years of taking care of an ill relative, tenderly navigating a difficult relationship, or relying on God's rest to get you through when you don't know what's ahead. But take heart, you are not alone. "For I am the Lord your God who takes hold of your right hand and says to you, Do not fear; I will help you" (Isaiah 41:13).

Seasons come and go as the circumstances of our lives change. How do we react to seasons of uncertainty, deciding how to move forward when we can't see what's ahead? For those of us who have invited Jesus into our hearts and lives, we can approach it with truth of the Lord. "'For my thoughts are not your thoughts, neither are your ways my ways,' declares the Lord. 'As the heavens are higher than the earth, so are my ways higher than your ways and my thoughts than your thoughts'" (Isaiah 55:8–9). God has a plan we don't even know about.

How you respond to an untimely or impending occurrence in your life depends on what you know as truth. I found my ultimate truth when I placed my faith in Christ as a young child, praying alongside my father after church in my room, and I received Jesus's gift of eternal life. My strength is found in remembering he paid for my sin with his life, gifting me with eternal life (John 3:16).

> Jesus answered, "I am the way and the truth and the life. No one comes to the Father except through me." (John 14:6)

Forging our own "ruts" in the road can feel successful in the moment. Or it can be a slippery slope where we crash and burn as we take God out of the picture. But what peace there is in approaching the Father for help! Discovering the ruts he has laid out ahead of us on icy roads makes difficult circumstances and unforeseen seasons more manageable.

> Looking to Jesus, the founder and perfecter of our faith, who for the joy that was set before him endured the cross, despising the shame, and is seated at the right hand of the throne of God. Consider him who endured from sinners such hostility against himself, so that you may not grow weary or fainthearted. (Hebrews 12:2–3 ESV)

When we lean on God's wisdom, strength, and guidance, he leads us to opportunities to see him work. He shows us how to travel through difficult seasons, down roads we never expected. And hopefully we recognize our journeys are all for his glory.

I made it safely to the store and back on that icy day, thankful for my father's words, direction, and love in showing me the ropes of how to drive in treacherous conditions. Imagine how much more the Father in heaven loves you.

Reflecting on God's Faithfulness

Faithful Before: Can you look back and see where God has walked with you through a season of uncertainty? Write about it here, thanking him for his goodness.

_____
_____
_____
_____

His Word: Read James 1:2–6 and Matthew 7:7–11. Write out what God says he will do when we ask.

_____
_____
_____
_____

Faithful Again: Are you currently searching for direction due to uncertainty in your future? Write out a prayer, asking God to remind you of his presence and the promise of Jeremiah 29:11–13.

_____
_____
_____
_____

#faithfulbeforefaithfulagain   DAY 14: Faithful in Uncertainty

Day Fifteen

A joyful heart is the inevitable result of a heart burning with love. She gives most who gives with joy.

—Mother Teresa[19]

Day 15

Faithful in Joy

Wedding bells were on the horizon, as we were busy with preparations for our second daughter's big day. My bestie graciously offered to host her bridal shower in her home, along with some other friends and family. At the time, mask mandates had been downgraded to optional, but to lessen the number of guests at one time and reduce the risk of exposing grandparents, our friends devised a plan to split the guests into two groups. My friend Stacey basically hosted two showers in her home, back-to-back on the same day.

She laid out a beautiful tablescape full of yummy treats for the room, which was filled with family, friends, and gifts for the newlyweds to be. The shower also included time to pray for the bride and groom and for God's blessing on the beginning of their upcoming marriage. It was truly beautiful!

Until the horrifying happened. I overflowed the toilet.

Suffice it to say, it was bad. I was dying inside, horrified at the prospect of walking into a room of lingering family and friends to somehow quietly explain the disintegrating situation down the hall. Thankfully, most of the guests had made their exit and only close family remained before I had excused myself to the restroom. I could hear my friend and the hostesses cleaning up from brunch, but what in the world should I do? It was probably the one time in my life that I didn't have my cell phone on me. I knew what I had to do. I snuck back unobtrusively into the living room, pulled Stacey away from cleaning up one mess to another, and told her what had happened. It was so embarrassing.

In stealth-like recovery, she slipped out of the room and cleaned up the mess, not allowing me to help since I was still "playing mother of the bride," as she said. Did I mention I was mortified? Stacey never said a word. She never threw me under the bus or shared this hilarity with the remaining people in her house.

Not only had she beautifully hosted a shower for my daughter, attended to every need of each guest, *and* cleaned up my embarrassing situation in silence and grace, she also went straight to work afterward. As a flight attendant, she had received a call during the shower and was due to check in for flight duty within two hours after the shower. Stacey accomplished it all with a spring in her step, a smile on her face, and a song in her heart. She did it all with overflowing joy! (Too soon?)

A consistent perspective of joy doesn't come naturally to me. I'm a planner. I like my ducks in a row, and woe to the man who ever knocks one out of line! I don't fly by the seat of my pants, and flexibility is something God is currently adding to my wheelhouse. It's not that the joy of Christ doesn't make me happy; it's that in the event of a situation, I usually see the problem first.

The last several years have helped me realize my patterns of anxiety. I never truly considered my behaviors or reactions as anxiety. I just thought, *Doesn't everyone worry about things like I do?* I still wonder sometimes why others don't let problems bother them in the same way. How on earth does that work?

It wasn't until I sat with the concept that I noticed this friend's constant encouragement, wisdom, and joyful perspective. Her outlook and demeanor consistently pointed me to Jesus and the positive way to look at things. "Rejoice in the LORD and be glad, you righteous; sing, all you who are upright in heart!" (Psalm 32:11). I knew God was telling me, "Choose joy, Lynn."

My reactions and decisions in times of stress, or in this case, the unimaginably embarrassing, are still my choice.

In the short four-chapter book of Jonah, after being instructed to go to Nineveh with a warning from God, Jonah decides to run away to Tarshish instead. But that didn't stop God's ultimate plan. After boarding a boat, in hopes of escape, Jonah was soon the cause of a different turbulence. God sent a storm that rocked the whole boat. Distressed crewmembers discovered Jonah's disobedience was the cause and threw him overboard. Jonah was swallowed by a giant fish, spit out after three days, and graciously saved by God. Back on dry land, he received the same instruction a second time and finally did what God asked of him. He went to Nineveh and proclaimed the message that God was going to destroy the city. Jonah watched the king of Nineveh and all the people repent, and God was merciful. "When God saw what they did and how they turned from their evil ways, he relented and did not bring on them the destruction he had threatened" (Jonah 3:10).

Such great news! Right? They repented and turned to the Lord. All was seemingly well. Here's the funny part about Jonah's reaction. He got mad. Not only did he get mad, Jonah threw himself a little pity party. He left town and sat in the shade, waiting "to see what would happen to the city," after telling God, "I knew that you are … a God who relents from sending calamity" (Jonah 4:5, 2).

Our perspective to a given situation is everything. Do we look back and see God's past faithfulness, or do we pout about the grossness of the smell of the fish that saved our life? We can be selfish, regretful, and jealous, muttering, "I told you so," to the one who knows it all already. Or we can be thankful to God for sparing our life, although we basically ran right into the fish's mouth in the first place.

> You turned my wailing into dancing; you removed my sackcloth
> and clothed me with joy. (Psalm 30:11)

Stacey would be the first to tell you that she's not perfect. But God has used her joyful spirit to show me joy is a choice. Day in and day out, a joyful perspective is an opportunity to believe that what God above has provided for us in the past, he will do again. It's a chance to share with the people around us that we trust in our Savior so we can experience joy, even in the waiting.

Even if the waiting includes a cleanup on aisle two!

Reflecting on God's Faithfulness

Faithful Before: Has there been a time in your life when you were able to find joy in the middle of a difficult situation? Write about how God provided you a joyful perspective.

_____

_____

_____

_____

His Word: Read James 1:2–3. What does Scripture say about how we are to react to trials?

_____

_____

_____

_____

Faithful Again: Are you currently struggling to see the joy God has for you in the middle of this season? Write out Romans 15:13 below and ask God to renew the joy of your salvation, turning you to the hope in Christ.

_____

_____

_____

_____

#faithfulbeforefaithfulagain

Day Sixteen

You don't drown by falling into
water, you only drown
if you stay there.

—Zig Ziglar[20]

Day 16

Faithful in Baggage

I'm not a natural observer of others in public, but my husband enjoys casually taking in the social interactions around us. He's a people watcher. We often joke about how I thoughtfully position myself at a restaurant table. I typically choose my seat so he faces away from the distractions of our fellow diners and TVs, allowing him to solely focus on me. Genius, right?

But when it comes to families, I get sucked into people watching too. Maybe it's the exhilarating freedom and exuberant love of life seen in small children, or perhaps it is watching how parents react to their kids. But I love a good conversation between parent and child. Observing a teachable moment in action is almost as good as being a part of one!

One of my favorites happened while I lounged on the beach. We arrived early that morning, but several hours later other families began crashing our morning solitude. Kids ran ahead of their parents, excited to jump and splash in the ocean. Moms and grandparents carried backpacks, bags, or younger children, while dads were stuck toting coolers and figuring out how to correctly assemble pop-up tents for respite from the afternoon sun.

In this instance, a father with his two small children, a little boy and his sister, made a home base next to us. Dad never left them alone, watching in the wings. He let them roam within reason, remaining there to help guide them with a quick word or redirection to the safe zone of their staked spot for the day.

After settling in, his little loves played on the beach, occasionally sticking their toes in the cold water. The little boy would drag his bucket, fill it with sand, and dump it out as soon as it was full. Then he would do it again. Over and over he poured shells, sand, and an occasional candy wrapper into what was becoming a large mound of sand and treasures. He loved all these findings and had to keep everything he discovered!

A few minutes into their bucket brigade, the little girl squealed with delight as she poured out the contents of her bucket in front of her father. I heard her say in a rather shocking fashion, "Daddy, I caught a fish!" Much to her father's surprise, she *did* catch a fish, albeit a dead one. From where I sat, it looked like a tiny dead baby shark. But in reality, they all look like sharks to me. Hence, the reason I was on the shore!

Not causing any alarm, the dad calmly proceeded to help them bury whatever kind of dead fish it was and shooed the kids back off to play. No sooner had the two children splashed in the ocean than the little girl began to complain about something stinging. She reappeared on their blanket with the red splotchy markings from a jellyfish that had made contact with the back of her calf.

Clearly turning into a less-than-relaxing day at the beach, the dad began looking for a way out. Quick-minded, due to their short attention span and the increasing whining from the jellyfish sting, he said, "You guys wanna go to the pool?" *Distraction*, I thought and giggled under my breath. Genius parenting in action.

"Yay!"

The little boy, maybe three or four years old, came back to help clean up their toys and belongings. After a few trips from his mound of treasure to the bags they brought, he dropped to his knees, moaning. Overwhelmed by the realization that his toy fishing net was too heavy with sand, he gave up the work ahead and cried.

"Just load your toys in the cart," Dad said.

"I can't leave my net, and it's too heavy for me to pick up," the little boy said. The thought of leaving behind all he had been through that morning was too much for him. He didn't want to dig through the mound to find his treasure of toys. He wanted to just take it all. The heat was draining the joy right out of him and proving more than he could bear. He sat in the sand, head buried in his hands, crying, "It's too heavy; I can't leave it here!"

In unimaginable calmness, Dad lowered to one knee in front of his son, moved one hand, looked him in the eye, and said, "Son, just leave it here. Dump it out and only take your treasure."

Problem solved, the boy's demeanor changed, and his tears dried up. His self-inflicted problem of holding on to more than he could carry lightened immediately upon his father's alternate solution. He could simply leave what was weighing him down.

Oh, how my heart absorbed the simplicity of the answer lovingly offered to his downcast son. Tears turned into a slight smile as he realized he could take his net and treasures to his new adventure at the pool and leave the "baggage" behind at the beach.

Sometimes in our daily walk with Christ, we can get overwhelmed with the problems of the here and now, thinking we are solely responsible for solutions. Our self-reliance and "I can do it" attitude get in the way. We let problems, past decisions, or experiences deter us, instead of seeking the Father's guidance.

I've heard some people say we should not go to God with our problems because he is busy and we should not take up his valuable time. His care in solving world issues *must* trump the baggage of sand I can't filter through. But that couldn't be further from the truth. The truth of God's Word says otherwise.

> Come to me, all you who are weary and burdened, and I will give you rest. Take my yoke upon you and learn from me, for I am gentle and humble in heart, and you will find rest for your souls. For my yoke is easy and my burden is light. (Matthew 11:28–30)

> Humble yourselves, therefore, under God's mighty hand, that he may lift you up in due time. Cast all your anxiety on him because he cares for you. (1 Peter 5:6–7)

It can be difficult to let go of things that weigh heavy on our hearts, whether past or present. Life's challenges can make us wish for a lighter load. But we are not meant to be dragged down by our burdens and walk through life alone. God came to give us life and cares so much for us. He would leave the crowds of many, just for one. Just for you. And he did. We can trust him with our bags of sand.

> What do you think? If a man owns a hundred sheep, and one of them wanders away, will he not leave the ninety-nine on the hills and go to look for the one that wandered off? And if he finds it, truly I tell you, he is happier about the one sheep than about the ninety-nine that did not wander off. In the same way your Father

in heaven is not willing that any of these little ones should perish. (Matthew 18:12–14)

As believers, we have hope in Christ our Savior and joy in knowing there is nothing our God can't do. And when we spend time with him each day, we can find peace, rest, and comfort in letting him carry our load.

Reflecting on God's Faithfulness

Faithful Before: Can you remember a time you held on to past baggage God wanted to carry for you? Write about it here, thanking him for his goodness.

_____
_____
_____
_____

His Word: Reread Matthew 11:28–30 and 1 Peter 5:6–7, then write what you learn about God's heart for us.

_____
_____
_____
_____

Faithful Again: Is there something currently weighing you down? Write out a prayer, naming the baggage, and ask the Father to remind you of his presence now and to give you relief to whatever is weighing you down.

_____
_____
_____
_____

#faithfulbeforefaithfulagain

DAY 16: Faithful in Baggage

Day Seventeen

Forgiveness is not an occasional act; it is a constant attitude.

—Martin Luther King, Jr.[21]

Day 17

Faithful in Forgiveness

A new desk calendar for a brand new month means a fresh start. A clean slate. Call me old-school, but the visual of tasks, special dates, and a monthly overview rank right up there with a new planner! An empty, untouched thirty-day road map in the center of my desk brims with possibilities.

The prior month had been ridiculously busy, filled with all that comes from starting a full-time job, multiple personal events, and a plethora of details yet unsorted in my brain. The desire to empty those details from my head and onto paper is a dream that a list-maker like myself fully embraces. But by the end of that month, I was ready to turn the page.

You can imagine my disgust when, while eating spaghetti at my desk, I dropped a blob of marinara on my perfectly clean, white calendar. On the first of the month, no less! I swear, I would never unsee that spot again. Once white with the promise of future accomplishments, this stain was now a glaring reminder of a thoughtless misstep. For the next thirty days, my eyes would see nothing but that icky red circle. That saucy blemish on my sparkling month of promise would stare a hole through my uptight soul.

I love how God uses the simple things in our lives to speak truth to our hearts. He's so good like that. In his quiet whispering way, he immediately reminded me of several things in this inconsequential lunchtime experience.

At first, the stain was all I saw. The past unfortunate mistake immediately became my focus and I became hyper-fixated on it. Perspective is everything. We have a choice in our responses: move on, sit and pout, or repeat any given action. One of my favorite verses speaks volumes to how the Father wants to fill our hearts and minds.

> Finally, brothers, whatever is true, whatever is honorable, whatever is just, whatever is pure, whatever is lovely, whatever is commendable, if there is any excellence, if there is anything worthy of praise, think about these things. (Philippians 4:8 ESV)

Focusing on the negative can get in the way of forward progress, much like sin can impede our spiritual growth. I realize we are talking about spaghetti sauce here, an accident that means nothing to my everyday life. Yet it illustrates how sin can burrow deep, grow, and distract us from God's mission for us.

As time went on, that blob proved just another spot on my desk calendar. The funny thing is, as much as that stain tormented me the first few days, its effect on me lessened daily in the ensuing weeks. I became used to its presence and barely noticed it was there—so much so that I let it happen again the next month! (Same situation, different food. Clearly I shouldn't eat at my desk.)

I could have turned the desk calendar over. I could have covered it with paper towels or simply chosen to eat somewhere else. But I didn't. I would remember and be careful next time, right? Surely, I could control my actions?

Apparently not.

What peered back at me in this new tangible word picture was sin and God's forgiveness. We can get comfortable with sin. Did that little spot bother me as much at the end of the month as it did at the beginning? Hardly. It became a nuisance, reflecting laziness, maybe even pride, by the fact that I did it again. But no, it was not near as impactful by day twenty-six. Along the way, not only had the spot remained, it also bled through to the page below. It affected the pages surrounding it, even absorbing any other dirt that maneuvered its way to my desk. Little by little over the course of the full thirty days, it grew.

Sin is sneaky, seeping in a little at a time, slowly numbing our hearts and minds to its effects. Isn't that the Enemy's plan (John 10:10)? Before we know it, our vibrant pursuit for Christlikeness has become commonplace. New sin becomes old sin that blends into the surroundings. Obviously, this eating faux pas wasn't a sin. But to me, it represented sin slipping into my life, affecting my choices and unnoticed in the end. A nasty attitude, words spoken in harsh, quick anger, a white lie supposedly to protect someone. Sin digs its roots deep, propagating its presence and widening its reach. Something that stains is costly, but God's gracious gift provides invaluably more.

> For the wages of sin is death, but the free gift of God is eternal life in Christ Jesus our Lord. (Romans 6:23 ESV)

We are faced with many obstacles on a daily basis this side of heaven, and we have to make choices as to whom we will serve and who will advise us in our decision-making. When it comes to opportunities to sin, God's Word encourages us:

> Be sober-minded; be watchful. Your adversary the devil prowls around like a roaring lion, seeking someone to devour. (1 Peter 5:8 ESV)

Do we recognize areas where sin stains, not bringing glory to God? Have we carved out space for something now so habitual that we've forgotten its presence undermines the heart of God's plan for us? Can God's desired holiness ring above the noise of everyday life? What do we do when we miss the mark?

Forgiveness.

> Whoever conceals their sins does not prosper, but the one who confesses and renounces them finds mercy. (Proverbs 28:13)

Confession leads to renouncing sin, ending in God's forgiveness and mercy. This is so much more than a messy working lunch. God's whisper to my heart wasn't about the blob on my calendar. It was about his next clean month. Forgiveness is offered through our confession to the Father. The new month is there for the taking, by simply pulling the corner and tearing the old away in confession to our God who is "faithful and just and will forgive us our sins and purify us from all unrighteousness" (1 John 1:9).

A clean slate. Forgiveness and mercy we don't deserve, but the free gift we can enjoy.

Reflecting on God's Faithfulness

Faithful Before: Can you remember a time when the forgiveness of God was so apparent? Write about it here, thanking him for his goodness to walk with you.

_____
_____
_____
_____

His Word: Read John 3:16, Romans 6:23, and 1 John 1:8–10. Write out what God reveals about sin and forgiveness.

_____
_____
_____
_____

Faithful Again: Are you currently sitting in a season of sin? Write out a prayer thanking God for his forgiveness before and asking him to forgive you now.

_____
_____
_____
_____

Day Eighteen

Behind every great child is a mom who's pretty sure she's screwing it all up.

—Anonymous[22]

Day 18

Faithful in Imperfection

As much as he missed his sisters, our final child at home relished the solitude as the sole upstairs resident. Who doesn't love ownership of the remote and hot water that doesn't turn cold mid-shower? But it wasn't long before this newfound freedom led him to campaign for a dog.

Much to my chagrin, we agreed and bought a puppy a few months later, beginning a sweet, yet hairy, relationship with our now seventy-pound goldendoodle, Maverick. As he grew, there would be occasional reminders of his early training days—a holey sock here, a chewed-up pillow corner there, a trail of toilet paper strung down the hall. But one particular remnant of puppydom hit me differently.

Stepping outside for a walk on a chilly day, I grabbed my favorite walking jacket. As I stuffed my hands deep into my pockets, there it was. My right hand went completely through the bottom of the pocket. I turned the pocket inside out, recognizing a tear made only by none other than that now-grown puppy. It was my favorite jacket, and the hole in the pocket bugged me. Maybe I should just get rid of it or try and sew it closed. But the hole did not affect the jacket's ability to provide warmth. Over that chilly season, that hole prompted reflections on my own shortcomings.

Oh, you know the ones—thoughts and doubts that often plague a mother's heart, mind, and soul. Fear that I wasn't doing enough. Or maybe I was doing too much. Or how I was going to adjust to an empty nest.

Was the jacket like my life, marked and less than perfect, with hidden signs of missteps? Yes. But it was still useful to the one who paid for it.

The Bible is full of examples of people whom God used. Some in simple ways and others in amazing ways. Some had less-than-stellar reputations, with sins we might consider unthinkable. They were marked and surely unworthy. But God sees us differently. Scripture tells us God looks at the heart, as he told Samuel about David. "But the LORD said to Samuel, 'Do not consider his appearance or his height, for I have rejected him. The LORD does not look at the things people look at. People look at the outward appearance, but the LORD looks at the heart'" (1 Samuel 16:7).

Being useful to God has nothing to do with our abilities, inabilities, weaknesses, or sins. No hole in our past or failure in our present changes how God looks at us. He can use believers who have put their faith in him to show the world his love *because* of what he has done in their lives. We learn to see the power in his grace poured out in our mistakes, allowing us to share with others how he has worked in us.

Hebrews 11 is known as the "hall of faith" chapter. It describes individuals used because of their faith in God, despite their imperfections and weaknesses. Let's look at a few examples:

Rahab was a prostitute. God used Rahab anyway. She believed in God and his power to protect her while hiding his men (Joshua 2, Hebrews 11:31) and was noted in the lineage of Christ (Matthew 1).

Moses was chosen to lead the children of Israel out of slavery and train up a successor in Joshua. Moses killed a man in anger (Exodus 2:11–12). He later sinned and was not allowed to enter the promised land despite delivering the Israelites (Exodus 3:10, Exodus 20). God used Moses anyway.

David was anointed king as a young teen shepherd. Once king, he committed adultery with the wife of a subordinate, then in order to cover up his sin, sent her husband to his death. God used David anyway. David gave us many psalms, is known as a "man after God's own heart," and is named in the lineage of Christ (1 Samuel 16, 2 Samuel 11, and Matthew 1:6).

Abraham was promised a son. Yet his impatience led him to follow his wife's advice, and he slept with his wife's maid in order to provide an heir. God used Abraham anyway. God later fulfilled his promise of a son (true heir), and he also implemented a covenant. God promised to bless Abraham's descendants—as many as the stars in the sky and sands of the sea (Genesis 16:1–4, Genesis 22, and James 2:23).

Paul persecuted Christians before he became a Christ follower, even watching the martyrdom of the church leader Stephen. God used Paul anyway. God used Paul's conversion to reach Gentiles and to write multiple books of the New Testament.

My kids' youth pastor used to say, "Christ came to do what we can never do for ourselves." He came to forgive our sins and mistakes, declaring us righteous when we accept his love and forgiveness through faith. Our usefulness and value to God have nothing to do with our mistakes or past missteps and everything to do with a Father who shows us grace. We can clean ourselves up and mend the holes to appear more worthy to the naked eye, but the grace of the gospel is that we don't deserve it. God offers it anyway. "For God so loved the world that he gave his one and only Son, so that whoever believes in him shall not perish but have eternal life" (John 3:16).

For those of us who have asked Christ into our hearts and have accepted his forgiveness, he gives us the promise of a future and hope. "'For I know the plans I have for you,' declares the Lord, 'plans to prosper you and not to harm you, plans to give you hope and a future. Then you will call on me and come and pray to me, and I will listen to you. You will seek me and find me when you seek me with all your heart'" (Jeremiah 29:11–13).

As moms, some mistakes cause us to doubt our decisions. We often beat ourselves up as our parenting styles mature. *Why did I yell? Will my harsh, angry words affect their little hearts forever? I'm the adult, shouldn't I exhibit more patience and kindness?*

But who said we're supposed to have it down on day one? Our mistakes are not an indictment against our ability to mother well. The question is: Am I running after God with my whole heart, asking for forgiveness when necessary, and moving forward in hope? What did I learn from missing the mark? And do I extend grace to others, even my children, in their own mistakes?

We still have our sweet, attention-seeking dog, and he's long since learned a thing or two. He no longer chews on furniture or clothes. We don't hold his past transgressions against him, and we love him in spite of what he does or doesn't do. I started to replace and repair some of those items, which bore visible marks of his past puppy indiscretions. But they serve as a sweet reminder of the extended grace and forgiveness of God to my imperfect heart.

Sweet momma, sharing with our children how much God loves us and can use us despite ourselves is a personal story full of God's goodness, forgiveness, and love. And I can think of no better lesson to share with your kids.

So I wear my jacket on a cold day, dig my hands deep into my pockets, and smile at the hole at the bottom, thankful for God's grace.

Reflecting on God's Faithfulness

Faithful Before: Can you look back and see where God has been faithful to you despite your imperfections or past sin? Write about it here, thanking him for his goodness.

_____

_____

_____

_____

His Word: Write out 1 Samuel 16:7 in your favorite Bible translation (e.g. NIV, ESV, MSG).

_____

_____

_____

_____

Faithful Again: Are you currently struggling with the concept of God using you because of an area you haven't surrendered to him? Read Jeremiah 31:3 and write out a prayer asking him to remind you of his presence and unconditional love.

_____

_____

_____

_____

#faithfulbeforefaithfulagain

Day Nineteen

The point is that each person's pride is in competition with everyone else's pride. It is because I wanted to be the big noise at the party that I am so annoyed at someone else being the big noise.

—C. S. Lewis[23]

Day 19

Faithful in Pride

We splurged on a celebratory trip to the Dominican Republic for our thirtieth anniversary. This was our first trip out of the country since having children, so we had a lot to catch up on. Scuba diving, swimming with dolphins, and snorkeling topped our list … well Reggie's list. He was open to anything. I, on the other hand, was not. My idea of a great vacation was a chair, a book, and clean water for a nearby dip when the sun became too much. I finally acquiesced, fully giving in to the familial pressure to get out and enjoy God's creation. In other words, I agreed to get out of my comfort zone.

We relaxed for a week in an all-inclusive resort, something we had never done. While on a boat excursion, Reggie coerced me into climbing to the top deck to watch the view as we motored back to shore. On the way down, I slipped as I stepped down from the ladder. My foot went one way, and my big toe went the opposite direction. I was sure something was broken. Romantic, I know. Excruciating as it was to walk on, and with only two days remaining on our trip, I hobbled around, leaning on my husband for support.

When we arrived home, a doctor confirmed my foot was indeed broken. But a week later, I woke up unable to turn my neck to the left. At all. The next few weeks proved to be more than a crick in my neck from sleeping on it funny. Driving was downright nerve-racking, and changing lanes was a monumental task.

Thankfully, an MRI revealed only soft tissue damage. It would heal in time, but I still needed physical therapy. I did the exercises, slowly regaining the ability to once again feel safe merging into traffic. The annoyance from restricted movement eventually lessened the more I regained my ability to see my surroundings clearly.

God's description of the Israelites as "stiff-necked" quickly became much more understandable to me. "'I have seen these people,' the LORD said to Moses, 'and they are stiff-necked people'" (Exodus 32:9). My inability to turn around was one thing, brought on by an accident, but what caused God to describe the Israelites this way?

Jeremiah was a prophet in the Old Testament. God spoke to him about the condition of Israel and their rebellious hearts, often using Jeremiah to speak to the people regarding their stiff-necked behavior. God repeatedly admonished them for their disobedience. They faced forward, unwilling to turn back to God. "Yet they did not listen or pay attention; they were stiff-necked and would not listen or respond to discipline" (Jeremiah 17:23).

Was it pride? Self-reliance? Were they so focused on where they were going, forging their own path, that they wouldn't stop to turn to God, listening for his direction or desire for them? The Israelites had developed a pattern of thanking God for whatever miracle, deliverance, or provision the day brought. They would praise him and pledge their devotion. They would worship and give their sacrifices, but it rarely lasted long.

How soon we forget!

Many times in the book of Judges, you see phrases like, "And children of Israel did what was right in their own eyes" or "The Israelites did evil in the eyes of the LORD." God sent judges to expose their prideful and sinful hearts (Judges 2:11; 3:7, 12; 4:1; 6:1; 13:1).

> But when the judge died, the people returned to ways even more corrupt than those of their ancestors, following other gods and serving and worshiping them. They refused to give up their evil practices and stubborn ways. (Judges 2:19)

The same is true of many of the kings noted in 1 and 2 Kings. God placed them on the throne, but many of them were filled with pride and selfishness, reigning in their own power. Many of the kings' legacies are remembered as "evil in the eyes of the LORD," such as King Jehoahaz (2 Kings 13:2) and King Jehoash (2 Kings 13:11).

I'm not throwing shade on the stories of the Old Testament, as if to indicate I don't also have moments of pride or relying on myself. Refusing to be moldable when convicted by the Holy Spirit exposes a heart full of pride. And living a life in self-reliance can lead to eliminating a need for God. Such a forward, prideful attitude means we need to turn around, face the Father for his opinion, and repent for leaving him out of the picture.

Self-reliance is a theme in today's culture … living life how you want, doing things your way, living your "best life." That's a lot of *you*. Are we more concerned with living to make ourselves happy? Or are we filtering our actions through the hands of the Father who created us for his honor and glory, and not our own? The Bible tells us that God should be the focus of all we do. "So whether you eat or drink or whatever you do, do it all for the glory of God" (1 Corinthians 10:31).

Christ followers don't always get it right. We are sinners but forgiven, broken but in the process of healing. The sole intent of following the one who died and forgave us, even though we fail him over and over, is to live to honor him. We do that through our actions, inactions, baby steps, big steps, ups, and downs, while we volunteer at school, parent our children, decide the next steps in our business, navigate our relationships, and make our plans. Having a full range of motion to turn to see the Savior's perspective is everything!

When we follow Christ's leading, we become more in tune with the Father, which allows us to walk forward in godly confidence. "And whatever you do, whether in word or deed, do it all in the name of the Lord Jesus, giving thanks to God the Father through him" (Colossians 3:17).

Reflecting on God's Faithfulness

Faithful Before: Can you remember a season where your pride kept you from letting God lead you? Write about it here, thanking him for his goodness to walk with you.

_____

_____

_____

_____

His Word: Jeremiah 17:5–8 shows a sharp contrast between those who relied on themselves—stiff-necked and focused on their own path—and those who looked to God. Fill in the chart below with descriptions of the two kinds of people referred to in this passage.

SELF-RELIANT	RELIANT ON GOD

Faithful Again: Are you currently relying on yourself more than God? Write out a prayer asking him to forgive you and direct your next steps.

_____

_____

_____

_____

#faithfulbeforefaithfulagain

Day Twenty

You just stay in this one corner of the forest waiting for others to come to you. Why don't you come to them sometimes?

—A. A. Milne[24]

Day 20

Faithful in Intentionality

There is not much more annoying than talking to someone who is distracted. Teachers aim for active listening; parents call it paying attention. It's a skill we have lost in this modern era of accessibility, with information always at our fingertips, dividing our attention and overloading our minds. Intentionality causes us to live in the moment but takes more effort than the days of our youth.

I recently made a quick run to the local Trader Joe's market, as the holidays were fast approaching. Getting ahead is my superpower. After working retail and parenting three phone-obsessed teenagers, I don't like to scroll on my device when I'm checking out. Engaging in conversation with someone new, who is doing their job on my behalf, seems the least I can do. My phone call, text, or social app perusal can wait.

"What are you most excited about in your cart?" the young woman at the register asked. Wow, what a great question! I had never been asked that at the store, but it took our chat to a whole new level. I responded with a couple of items I had picked up for my niece's son—animal crackers, cookies, just a couple of small treats any two-year-old would love. We were taking them dinner at the end of the week. When the checker asked why I chose those items, I proceeded to tell her about their recent adoption, which then led to a back-and-forth discourse on the high cost of adoption. Then the Lord reminded me of a story I could share to bring him into the conversation, which is always a favorite opportunity!

My niece and her husband had taken advantage of a foundation started by friends called One More Ministries. This foundation offers adoption funding for couples who feel led to answer God's call to care for orphans and widows (James 1:27, Matthew 25:40, 45). As my conversation with the cashier ended, she wrapped up by saying how great organizations like One More Ministries are, so couples can provide forever homes to children with no families. As I agreed wholeheartedly, she took the receipt out of the registered printer, looked me directly in the eyes, and said, "To him be the glory."

Indeed!

When it comes to sharing God with people around us, we automatically assume their rejection will be of us, or that maybe they don't know the Father as we do. We can often be standoffish in mentioning our Savior's name, as it's become taboo and offensive. But when the Spirit moves in your heart, even just to be kind and engage a stranger in conversation, God responds. Each opportunity brings a reminder of a story or a verse or something we never imagined. And honestly, I did not expect her response.

In John 4, Jesus stops to rest on his journey back to Galilee, and he meets a Samaritan woman at a well. The Jews and Samaritans weren't exactly friendly (John 4:9). Additionally, men were unaccustomed to even speaking in public with women. Jesus asks her for a drink of water and eventually graciously offers himself, the Living Water. He even reveals himself as the Messiah for the first time. "Jesus answered, 'Everyone who drinks this water will be thirsty again, but whoever drinks the water I give them will never thirst. Indeed, the water I give will become in them a spring of water welling up to eternal life'" (John 4:13–14).

When his revelation fully sinks in, the woman realizes she is indeed talking to the Messiah prophesied for generations. Prompted by her belief and encounter with Christ, she takes the step we often struggle to take … she shared with others. "Then, leaving her water jar, the woman went back to the town and said to the people, 'Come, see a man who told me everything I ever did. Could this be the Messiah?' They came out of the town and made their way toward him" (John 4:28–30).

I love this commentary found in *Come and See: A Study on the Gospel of John* from The Daily Grace Co.:

> The testimony of the Samaritan woman made the townspeople want to know this man that she spoke of. They saw her life and then they came to him. They wanted to know more based on what they had seen from her. The text makes it clear that they did not believe because of her testimony, but because they came and learned who he was for themselves. Her testimony made them

curious and God used it to draw many to himself. Their hearts now tasted the goodness of the God that they saw in her.... Our stories do not have the power to save, but they do have the power to draw people to want to know more about who Jesus is.[25]

God's faithfulness in our intentions can be astounding or small. As ambassadors of Christ and through an awareness of the Holy Spirit's tug on our heart, we can be used to tell our own story and to share with others we meet. And it's a bonus when God reminds us of his love with a gentle nod that he is working on both sides of the register. Even at the grocery store.

Reflecting on God's Faithfulness

Faithful Before: Can you recall a time when God met you in your intentionality to be available to his leading? Write about it here, thanking him for his prompting.

_____
_____
_____
_____

His Word: Paraphrase John 4:39–41 below.

_____
_____
_____
_____

Faithful Again: Are you currently struggling with being intentional to share with others what God is doing in you? Write out a prayer, asking God to remind you of his presence now and in future opportunities.

_____
_____
_____
_____

#faithfulbeforefaithfulagain   DAY 20: Faithful in Intentionality

Day Twenty-One

Almost everything will work again if you unplug it for a few minutes, including you.

—Anne Lamott[26]

Day 21

Faithful in Encouragement

All three of our kiddos attended different universities, each school having its own vibe and cultural atmosphere and each with varying distance from home. But when you move away from home, the distance is inconsequential. You are still not home.

The challenge of newfound independence begins once the honeymoon phase of welcome week wears off. Some may feel homesick for the first time. There's a learning curve to figuring out how to manage all your classes, get yourself out of bed on time, and leave enough time to walk across campus, and direction and encouragement can be helpful occasionally. (And a great planner app never hurts!)

My husband and I felt strongly that our kids should move away to college, if they felt so inclined. We knew independent living would give them the opportunity to make their own decisions while also furthering their education. We still supported them financially, prayerfully, and emotionally, and the invisible safety net of home remained intact, should the need arise.

I saw this need especially around finals, and I was all-in with providing reinforcement through love and support from home. I took great joy in mailing an occasional care package with their favorite snacks, notecards for studying, and gift cards, knowing it provided joy on the receiving end as well. By our third child, as technology advanced, my husband was known to forward fast-food reward points to supplement cash flow shortages. (We learned through the years that cash was not always the best commodity for their not yet fully mature, soon-to-be-adulting selves.)

As you can imagine, each child was different, as was every situation. Where one child appreciated a text, another needed a phone call. Where one loved a handwritten note, one might need distance and time to marinate in a given situation. Recognizing the individuality in our children and the different scenarios called for varied approaches, and our strategies evolved over the years. My mom skills were challenged in the twelve years of putting three kids through college. Although each child faced different issues, with a myriad of requests and shared answers, our message as parents to these treasured gifts from God remained the same … we were there when and if they needed us. They only needed to ask.

When my third child was in college, I saw a Facebook post on a university parents' page about a mom who had written multiple letters to her child, each to a different end. Each envelope was sealed with a directive written across the front. One envelope said, "Open when you're sad." Others said, "Open when you miss me," "Open when you are angry," or "Open when you need a funny memory." Each letter could be opened at any time, depending on the student's need.

No sooner had I begun devising a strategy for carrying out this project to the current Nitcher in college did I hear the Holy Spirit whisper: "I did the same for you, you know." My encouragement from God came in a slightly different package—the Bible. God's Word is filled with letters from him, full of instruction, encouragement, love, admonishment, and wisdom, all pointing me to Christ. The Bible is the ultimate encouragement to my mom heart, right at my fingertips. And it's there for your encouragement too.

God was right, as always. I was cheering up my college student with letters from their mom who loved them endlessly. But how was I encouraging myself, as well as my child, to find peace, joy, and much-needed wisdom on a daily basis? What about my own heart? Where was I to go for encouragement and perspective when my eye-rolling teenager wasn't too fond of my parenting style?

My friends?

A self-help book?

Other moms?

None of these resources are inherently bad, and when filtered through a biblical lens, they can often be helpful. But the Bible is our ultimate source of help. And my motherly confidence is boosted when I look to the Bible as a collection of love letters to help meet my every need. It's not all up to me, thank the good Lord!

In the last chapter of Matthew, Jesus appeared to the disciples before he ascended to the right hand of God. He told them to go, teach, and tell the nations all they had seen, learned, and heard from him during his ministry. It's often called the Great Commission. To me, the best part of this instruction is his reminder that he will always be with them. "Therefore go and make disciples of all nations, baptizing them in the name of the Father and of the Son and of the Holy Spirit, and teaching them to obey everything I have commanded you. And surely I am with you always, to the very end of the age" (Matthew 28:19–20).

That's our task, mommas. Share with our kids what God has done for us and remind them of his good promise to always be there. His words are the ultimate encouragement, you can be sure!

Sometimes God moves in the simplest of ways. That day, he used a post on Facebook to remind me that the Bible contains letters of encouragement for all situations at just the right time. Much like an unopened envelope, intrinsic value and encouragement can be found in God's Word. Whether it's sitting on my nightstand or lying in the seat of my car, I just need to open it, and its treasures await:

> The LORD is my shepherd, I lack nothing. He makes me lie down in green pastures, he leads me beside quiet waters, he refreshes my soul. He guides me along the right paths for his name's sake. Even though I walk through the darkest valley, I will fear no evil, for you are with me; your rod and your staff, they comfort me. You prepare a table before me in the presence of my enemies. You anoint my head with oil; my cup overflows. Surely your goodness and love will follow me all the days of my life, and I will dwell in the house of the LORD forever. (Psalm 23)

Letters fashioned in love with instructions to "open when …" are so similar in purpose to our holy correspondence—letters bound back-to-back in our leather-wrapped treasure. The Bible is a book full of love letters from the Father, ever available, and waiting to comfort and encourage our souls.

Faithful in Encouragement

Reflecting on God's Faithfulness

Faithful Before: Can you look back and see a time when God used Scripture to encourage you? Write about it here, thanking him for his goodness.

_____

_____

_____

_____

His Word: Write out the action words from Psalm 23 that show the ways God loves and encourages you.

_____

_____

_____

_____

Faithful Again: Are you currently in need of encouragement yourself or ideas on ways to encourage your children? Write out a prayer asking God to remind you of his presence now, and commit to continue digging into Scripture in the week ahead.

_____

_____

_____

_____

#faithfulbeforefaithfulagain

Now What?

You did it! You completed this 21-day devotional challenge! So now what? You've begun a new habit, a daily discipline for studying God's Word, finding him #faithfulbeforefaithfulagain on a daily basis in the everyday situations of life. Seeing his faithfulness in our past challenges and messy situations encourages us as we encounter new difficult seasons.

Isn't it comforting to know you're not alone?

Now, in the words of my sweet hubby, *just keep going!* There are so many ways to make spending time with God a priority and part of your day! But they all require *action* on your part. Take a step and start somewhere. God will meet you there! Here are a few ideas:

Pray for God to show you where to start.
Ask God to send a friend to study the Bible with you.
Choose a time that is sustainable every day (but give yourself grace when you miss a day).
Journal about asked and answered prayers.
Listen to Scripture while you exercise or are in the car.
Jump into a group of women studying the Bible.
Sign up for a study led at your church or another Bible-teaching church near you.
Check out podcasts on the Bible or biblical motherhood.
Pick a Bible reading plan and read on your own (suggestions below).
Recruit an accountability partner to check in with.
Start a group in your own home and pick a book to study.
Meet with friends on Zoom or in person and study together.

Our seasons of motherhood change and require flexibility. Studying the Bible doesn't require being in your favorite chair, in total silence, with coffee in hand (although that's my second favorite). How often does *that* happen anyway? I literally started one of my most recent daily habits while drying my hair! Just begin somewhere!

Then, when you finish one study, find something else to study. Time in God's Word is transformational, affecting our attitudes and filling our hearts and minds with his truth.

Below are some of my favorite resources and female Bible teachers. Most of them also have a podcast. Their studies vary in length and depth and can usually be done in a group or on your own. I have found that *not every study fits in every season of motherhood,* and that's okay. In the words of my favorite Pilates instructor, Robin Long, "Find what works for you today." The options are endless!

The Daily Grace Co.: This is my current go-to Bible study publisher, with fantastic topic-based studies or studies on specific books of the Bible. I love studying on my own, and their sales are great, with prices as low as five or ten dollars. Their app is also helpful for study and reading plans. They also have a podcast!

Daily Reading Plan: I love *The Daily Grace Prayer Calendar: A Twelve Month Bible Study Companion*, by The Daily Grace Co. It includes a daily reading plan for the calendar year and an opportunity to journal asked and answered prayers each month. It also facilitates prayerfully planning of the month ahead. There is also an additional app specific to the day's reading.

Priscilla Shirer: All of Priscilla's studies are awesome and biblically sound. When purchasing her book through Lifeway, the company often sends a link to watch the video of her teaching. She's another fellow Texan, daughter of well-known pastor Dr. Tony Evans, and mom of three boys.

Christine Caine: One of my favorite Bible studies is Christine's *20/20 Vision. Seen. Chosen. Sent.* (This was the study I was doing when the world shut down.) Her evangelistic focus will challenge your heart!

Beth Moore: Beth is an amazing Bible teacher, with many great studies to choose from. She is a fellow Texan, mom of two girls, and grandmother to several grandchildren. She is a great storyteller.

Kay Arthur: Kay teaches a method of inductive Bible study through Precept Ministries, which teaches how to glean from Scripture. She has multiple types of studies, as well as a series of studies for children. (I refer to her as my grandmother in the faith, as her studies were the first studies I did as a young momma.) These studies are in-depth and longer than many others, but oh, so rich!

There are *tons* more, but these are devotionals and authors I have relied on through the years. I hope these are helpful! I'm so encouraged you've made it this far. God's Word is a force the Enemy can't compete with. Just keep going!

Consider yourself prayed for,

Lynn

Endnotes

1. Kevin Kruse, *"Stephen Covey: 10 Quotes That Can Change Your Life," Forbes*, July 16, 2012, https://www.forbes.com/sites/kevinkruse/2012/07/16/the-7-habits/?sh=5a44f87b39c6.
2. Katie Stiles, "45 Quotes about Anxiety," Psych Central, July 30, 2021, https://psychcentral.com/anxiety/quotes-about-anxiety#quotes-on-anxiety.
3. *Where the Crawdads Sing,* directed by Olivia Newman, (Culver City, CA: Sony Pictures Entertainment, 2022).
4. Charles H. Spurgeon, *Morning and Evening*, Goodreads, https://www.goodreads.com/quotes/tag/temptation?page=4.
5. A. A. Milne, *The Complete Tales of Winnie-the-Pooh*, Goodreads, https://www.goodreads.com/work/quotes/95547-winnie-the-pooh-the-house-at-pooh-corner.
6. Henry Kissinger, Goodreads, https://www.goodreads.com/quotes/306581-there-cannot-be-a-crisis-next-week-my-schedule-is.
7. "Matthew Henry Commentary of the Whole Bible (Concise) 1 Kings 19; vv. 9–13," Bible Study Tools, https://www.biblestudytools.com/commentaries/matthew-henry-concise/1-kings/19.html.
8. Ralph Waldo Emerson, Goodreads, https://www.goodreads.com/quotes/30537-our-chief-want-is-someone-who-will-inspire-us-to.
9. William Shakespeare, *Macbeth*, Goodreads, https://www.goodreads.com/quotes/1141939-present-fears-are-less-than-horrible-imaginings.
10. A. W. Tozer, *My Daily Pursuit: Devotions for Every Day*, "My Daily Pursuit Quotes," Goodreads, https://www.goodreads.com/work/quotes/26828096-my-daily-pursuit-devotions-for-every-day.
11. John M. Frame, "The Omnipotence, Omniscience, and Omnipresence of God," The Gospel Coalition, https://www.thegospelcoalition.org/essay/omnipotence-omniscience-omnipresence-god/.
12. Ann Landers, Goodreads, https://www.goodreads.com/quotes/17642-some-people-believe-holding-on-and-hanging-in-there-are.
13. The Chosen, Season Two, Episode 3, "Matthew 4:24," Co-Directed by Dallas Jenkins, Starring Jonathan Roumie, April 2021, Angel Studios, https://tinyurl.com/2s4jsvy8

14 Dillon Burroughs, *Hunger No More: A 1-Year Devotional Journey through the Psalms*, Goodreads, https://www.goodreads.com/work/quotes/22766331-hunger-no-more-a-1-year-devotional-journey-through-the-psalms.

15 Elisabeth Elliot, *Be Still My Soul: Reflections on Living the Christian Life*, Goodreads, https://www.goodreads.com/work/quotes/2558161-be-still-my-soul.

16 Helen Keller, Goodreads, https://www.goodreads.com/quotes/6017033-walking-with-a-friend-in-the-dark-is-better-than.

17 Kevin Kruse, *"Stephen Covey: 10 Quotes That Can Change Your Life," Forbes*, July 16, 2012, https://www.forbes.com/sites/kevinkruse/2012/07/16/the-7-habits/?sh=1d31813539c6.

18 Ralph Waldo Emerson, Goodreads, https://www.goodreads.com/quotes/6361-all-i-have-seen-teaches-me-to-trust-the-creator.

19 Mother Teresa, *In the Heart of the World: Thoughts, Stories and Prayers,* Goodreads, https://www.goodreads.com/work/quotes/1404196-in-the-heart-of-the-world-thoughts-stories-and-prayers.

20 Zig Ziglar, "Drowning," https://www.ziglar.com/quotes/drowning/.

21 Martin Luther King, Jr., "Draft of Chapter IV, 'Love in Action,'" Stanford, The Martin Luther King, Jr. Research and Education Institute, https://kinginstitute.stanford.edu/king-papers/documents/draft-chapter-iv-love-action.

22 Meagan, "71 Inspirational Mom Quotes," Mommy Travels (blog), https://mommytravels.net.

23 C. S. Lewis, *Mere Christianity*, Goodreads, https://www.goodreads.com/quotes/search?page=3&q=pride+c.s.+lewis.

24 A. A. Milne, "The House at Pooh Corner," *The Complete Tales and Poems of Winnie-the-Pooh* (New York: Dutton Children's Books, Penguin Random House), 314.

25 Kristin Schmucker, Aubrey Coleman, and Jana White, *Come and See: A Study of the Gospel of John* (The Daily Grace Co., 2017), 66.

26 Anne Lamott, "12 Truths I Learned from Life and Writing," Ted Talks, 2017, https://www.ted.com/talks/anne_lamott_12_truths_i_learned_from_life_and_writing/transcript.

ORDER INFORMATION

REDEMPTION PRESS

To order additional copies of this book, please visit
www.redemption-press.com.
Also available at Christian bookstores, Amazon, and Barnes and Noble.